The Correspondence of
GERARD MANLEY HOPKINS
and
RICHARD WATSON DIXON

Gerard Manley Hopkins
1880

The Correspondence

of

GERARD MANLEY HOPKINS

and

RICHARD WATSON DIXON

Edited with notes &
an Introduction
by

CLAUDE COLLEER ABBOTT

PROFESSOR OF ENGLISH LANGUAGE AND
LITERATURE IN THE UNIVERSITY OF
DURHAM

LONDON
OXFORD UNIVERSITY PRESS
NEW YORK   TORONTO

Oxford University Press, Ely House, London W. 1

GLASGOW NEW YORK TORONTO MELBOURNE WELLINGTON
CAPE TOWN SALISBURY IBADAN NAIROBI DAR ES SALAAM LUSAKA ADDIS ABABA
BOMBAY CALCUTTA MADRAS KARACHI LAHORE DACCA
KUALA LUMPUR SINGAPORE HONG KONG TOKYO

SBN 19 212115 4

FIRST PUBLISHED 1935
SECOND (REVISED) IMPRESSION 1955
REPRINTED 1970

PRINTED LITHOGRAPHICALLY IN GREAT BRITAIN
AT THE UNIVERSITY PRESS, OXFORD
BY VIVIAN RIDLER
PRINTER TO THE UNIVERSITY

PREFACE

THE letters written by Gerard Hopkins to Canon R. W. Dixon came into the possession of Robert Bridges about two years after Dixon's death on 23 January 1900. Bridges carefully arranged them in a large book, and noted at the beginning those he thought were of secondary importance as being mainly concerned with detailed criticism of Dixon's poems, many of which were never published. These letters he used in writing the memoir of Dixon that introduced a selection of the latter's poems; and they form one of the sources, D, for the text of the poems of Hopkins. Two letters have been added (Nos. XXXII and XLI). They were kindly lent by Mrs. Barnard, sister of the late Mrs. Dixon. The series, as will be seen, is still incomplete, but Mrs. Barnard could make no further addition. The loss of one letter in particular is much to be regretted—that giving Hopkins's considered verdict on *Mano*. This, I thought, might have been kept in Dixon's own copy of *Mano*, but that book is not in Mrs. Barnard's possession. When the page proofs of this volume had been returned Father J. H. Crehan, S.J., sent me word that in the library at Stonyhurst is a copy of *Mano* into which has been pasted the following undated note from Hayton, evidently written to Hopkins:

'Your letter crossed one that I sent to Stonyhurst. Many thanks for your delightful letter.

In extreme haste,
Ever yours
R. W. Dixon.'

The date is probably 13 August 1883. The book contains no remarks or pencillings by Hopkins.

These letters have been edited from photostats made by the O.U.P. They are printed in full (with one small exception—a repetition—noted in its place) even though a considerable number of the poems criticized in them cannot be traced.

Bridges thought that Dixon had himself destroyed these.[1] Mrs. Barnard tells me that she has no unpublished poems by Dixon, though 'after my sister's death all her papers were sent to me'. The chances, therefore, seem against their discovery. Yet my experience is that unless a paper is definitely known to have been destroyed it is well to assume that it may, possibly will, turn up later; and for this reason the letters are printed as they stand.

Fortunately most of the letters written by Dixon in answer to these were kept by Hopkins and are now in the possession of the Society of Jesus, to which Order, and to Mrs. Barnard, I am greatly indebted for permission to print them here. They also are given in full, and Dixon's spelling, including his erratic use of 'ſ', is followed. This series, first partially explored by Father Joseph Keating, S.J.,[2] is likewise incomplete, though the gaps are probably not serious. The gain in interest from being able to follow both sides of the correspondence is great. In order to facilitate reference the letters written by Hopkins are numbered consecutively, and those of Dixon have an A, or sometimes a B or even C added. Thus XII belongs to Hopkins, and the next two letters in date being written by Dixon are numbered XII A and XII B. Three contractions used in the footnotes to this volume are in place here:

C.C.: Christ's Company and other Poems, by R. W. Dixon, 1861.

H.O.: Historical Odes and other Poems, by R. W. Dixon, 1864.

S.P.: Poems by the late Rev. Dr. Richard Watson Dixon, a Selection with portrait and a Memoir by Robert Bridges, 1909.

The failure to trace Dixon's unpublished poems was not my only disappointment. The Very Rev. Dr. Henry Gee, dean of Gloucester, who passed the last two volumes of Dixon's *History*

---

[1] *S.P.*, p. 193.

[2] *The Month*, July, Aug., and Sept. 1909: 'Impressions of Father Gerard Hopkins, S.J.'; a very important contribution to the subject.

Preface

of the Church of England through the press, mentions in his Preface to vol. v a diary kept by the author, and makes some small use of it. He can, however, give me no information about it, so that my hope that it might supplement certain episodes in the letters is defeated. Mrs. Barnard can tell me nothing about it either. Nor has she an earlier photograph of Dixon that might have served as an additional illustration.

There is, however, one piece of good fortune to chronicle. While this book was passing through the press Miss Grace Hopkins made a further search among family papers in an attempt to discover the copies of Dixon's poems made by her brother.[1] It seemed possible that these might include some of the unpublished poems that he criticized. Miss Hopkins found the beautifully written copies, and allowed me to examine them. They are described in Appendix IV; but they contain only one unpublished poem.

Miss Hopkins found also at the same time something more important—a small bundle of her brother's music, which includes one or two compositions that give a better idea of his work in this kind than the examples quoted in the letters themselves. These are criticized in Appendix III by Mr. J. Dykes Bower, to whom I am much indebted for his interest.

In addition to the obligations alluded to above, I wish to thank Mr. A. P. White, Librarian of Highgate School, for information used in footnotes to the early letters. To Mr. Frederick Page's help I have already tried to pay tribute; and in the making of this volume Mrs. Robert Bridges has continued to be my helper and friend. C. C. A.

[1] See R. B.'s *Memoir* to *S.P.*, the Note on p. xlvi.

CONTENTS

LIST OF ILLUSTRATIONS

LIST OF LETTERS

BETWEEN G. M. H. AND R. W. D.

* Postcard.

List of Letters

INTRODUCTION

'THIS great ingenuous being went about among men almost unrecognized, though influencing nearly every one with whom he came in contact. As he respected every man, he won respect from all, and any lengthened intercourse with him awoke the best affinities of his associates, who became infected with his grace. . . . He was truly revered, and where he bestowed his affection the gift was so unmeasured that the mere flattery of it must have been injurious; were it not that spiritual love has no excess, but is always beneficent. It was more than any one could repay, and, however I have rejoiced in it, the remembrance, now that he is taken away, shames me with the thought of my unworthiness.' So writes Robert Bridges at the end of his memoir of Dixon, a prose tribute remarkable for its insight and reverence. The gracious and gentle spirit of Dixon shines out clearly from those affectionate recollections that must always be one of the few fields where knowledge of the shy poet-historian may be gathered. The emphasis throughout is on the man. He was a great gentleman and lovable. The testimony of the correspondence with Gerard Hopkins reinforces this judgement and adds greatly, by many a happy touch, to the savour of his mind and personality.

He was middle-aged when he entered the story of Bridges and Hopkins: 'a tallish, elderly figure, its litheness lost in a slight scholarly stoop, . . . wearing unimpeachable black cloth negligently, and a low-crowned clerical hat banded with twisted silk'. His early life, not well documented otherwise, must be inferred chiefly from his own memories of the friends of his youth, Burne-Jones, Morris, and Rossetti.[1] Both his mother and father were notable people: his father indeed, one of the leading

[1] The main documents for the life of Dixon, outside his poetry (rarely personal) and his *History*, are: R. B.'s *Memoir*; H. C. Beeching's article in *D.N.B.*; the preface to vol. v of his *History of the Church of England*; *Recollections of Dante Gabriel Rossetti*, by T. Hall Caine (1882); *Life of William Morris*, by J. W. Mackail (1889); *Memories of Edward Burne-Jones*, by G B-J. (1904); and the not very satisfactory article, *The Last Hermit of Warkworth*, by Mary Coleridge in *Non Sequitur* (1900).

Introduction

preachers and representatives of the Wesleyan Methodists at a time when that body was in friendly alliance with the Church of England, was a man of heroic type and unforgettable presence. His life was written by his son;[1] but this, though a full account, will be disappointing to those who may expect to find there self-revelation. It is rather a document of Methodism than a literary work, except perhaps in the last chapter where Dixon attempts a sketch of his father's character. The difference in temperament between father and son is well brought out by Bridges in a passage amply supported by other evidence (he has been speaking of James Dixon): 'The elder portraits of the poet are not unworthy of such parentage, yet the dignity, pathos, and serious melancholy of his features lacked the strength, attainment, and command, which made his father's aged head so magnificent.' A father so Olympian is difficult to live up to, yet the son, diffident and perhaps more finely tempered, in many ways resembled him.

The years spent at Oxford, however (he graduated in 1857), revealed to him the interests and purposes that were to govern his life. He went up to Pembroke College from King Edward VI School, Birmingham, where he was already a friend of Burne-Jones, and became a member of that Brotherhood whose fine enthusiasm and faith in beauty found immediate expression in *The Oxford and Cambridge Magazine*.[2] The inspiration of that time always remained with him. His remarks on Rossetti and Burne-Jones show how he idealized the friendships of those years: 'His friendship was of the sort that will not see a fault in a friend. It was absolutely generous and ideal, and would admit of no abatement whatever.'

Most members of the Brotherhood meant to take Orders, and Dixon persevered in this intention. Those intoxicating years at Oxford that passed all too quickly in the glamour of youthful endeavour were to be for long the brightest oasis in an outwardly uneventful life. A London curacy, succeeded by five years'

[1] *The Life of James Dixon, D.D., Wesleyan Minister*, 1874. His dates are 1788-1871.   [2] Jan.–Dec. 1856.

schoolmastering at Carlisle, led to the living of Hayton, a straggling village nearby, and the transition from a young man's dreams to the more prosaic business of life cannot always have been easy. So far as can be seen, Dixon surrendered little to circumstance. He had determined to be a poet and he continued to be a poet. What kind of schoolmaster he was there is now small means of knowing; he was certainly a devoted parish priest. Yet how greatly he feared the rut of routine and deadening of his intellectual life can be seen from what Bridges tells us of the manner in which *Mano* was composed; and there seems little doubt that he glances at his own case in this passage from the *Life* of his father: 'How many a poor minister of the Established Church, flung down for life on some bare hill-side, or in some unlettered hamlet, far from books, far from all intercourse that may tend to cheer and freshen his spiritual life, has reason to lament that something like 'the Methodist itinerancy is not embraced in the ecclesiastical system to which he belongs.'

To keep Accidie at bay he had another weapon besides poetry, the study of history. At Hayton was begun his monumental *History of the Church of England from the Abolition of the Roman Jurisdiction*, a work in six volumes (two of which were published after his death) that occupied most of his leisure for the rest of his life. For a parish priest with few immediate library facilities to plan and carry through a work on such a scale (he ranges from 1529 to 1570) is a magnificent achievement. If ever a book deserved to be called heroic, it is this. He aimed at writing a work of importance, and the spirit in which he set about the task is well seen in the letter to Hopkins of 22 June 1880, one of many references to the book: 'My aim is to get the exact truth, & give that, with whatever colour. I mean, that I do not pretend to be without prepossessions & bias; if I had not those, I should not take the labour of writing at all: but I hope never to be found supprefsing, telling half a story, concealing anything connected with any point at issue, or otherwise dealing dishonestly with materials. This is what I mean by historical honesty: not the having no bias or side.'

Introduction

Of the merits of the book as history, I cannot speak. When I have turned to it as a piece of prose the style has impressed me by its subtle personal flavour. The writing, easy, vivid, and picturesque, wears its learning lightly. A work of such magnitude, so ardently pursued, might well have seemed worthy of an official mark of esteem. Save from a few, however, it met with no considerable welcome. Dixon remained a country clergyman for the rest of his days. At the end of 1883 he was presented to the more congenial living of Warkworth in Northumberland, otherwise he held no post of distinction in the Church, except an honorary canonry at Carlisle and the office of rural dean. But Oxford, much to his pleasure, gave him recognition just before his death in 1900, in his sixty-seventh year.

Though official recognition was wanting, he had many distinguished friends, and unknown to himself his poetry had at least one fervent admirer in Gerard Hopkins, who from his early Oxford days had known his work intimately. The correspondence between the two poets starts, on a very different footing from that between Hopkins and Bridges, with a letter of admiration from a young priest of 33 to a country vicar of 45 who had for a little while been his schoolmaster; an unexpected letter so full of delicate understanding of his neglected verses that the older man, 'shaken to the very centre', opened like a flower to quickening praise that must have seemed like an act of God, coming as it did at a time of life when encouragement was doubly precious. Dixon had then been for about four years at Hayton. The friendship thus begun, maintained chiefly by letter, for they very seldom—probably only once—met, lasted till Hopkins's death, and meant much to both men. For Hopkins Dixon was not only a poet whose work had become part of his life. He came near to having the sanctity of mind that was even more important. 'This adds a charm to everything Canon Dixon writes, that you feel he is a gentleman and thinks like one,' he tells Bridges. This beauty of character is nowhere better seen than in his affectionate anxiety almost touching anguish lest Hopkins should renounce poetry. With Bridges he completes Hopkins's audience and is thus one of the main forces urging him to continue writing. To Dixon, as soon as he saw it, the poetry of the boy he dimly remembered came as a revelation. He knew at once he was in the presence of a gift that eclipsed his own, and he was quick to express his belief. On 5 April 1879 he writes: 'I have your Poems and have read them I cannot say with what delight, astonishment, & admiration. They are among the most extraordinary I ever read & amazingly original'; and characteristically suggests that, in order to arouse interest, he should mention them in an 'abrupt footnote' to the year 1540 in the next volume of his *History*. When this offer is gently declined he still wishes to do something, and rouses Hopkins to a flutter of distress by proposing to send the *Eurydice* to one of the Carlisle newspapers. But though the means to publication offered were unsuitable there is no doubt of the deep understanding of the man who writes (1 March 1880): 'in the power of forcibly & delicately giving the essence of things in nature, and of carrying one out of one's self with healing, these poems are unmatched.'

Such praise could not fail to have its effect. Yet, in a way, it is the older man who becomes the pupil, and the younger whose opinion is deferred to as the correspondence progresses. To Hopkins Dixon likewise owed the friendship of Bridges, Patmore's interest, and a detailed criticism of his own poems that was itself an act of devotion. That this criticism should bulk so largely in these letters to the exclusion of matters more generally interesting is a minor misfortune. Only occasionally can Dixon find time to give his own thoughts fully.

To attempt a short criticism of Dixon's poems after what Bridges and Hopkins have written need not, I think, seem presumptuous. Almost inevitably their views were partially coloured by friendship with the poet and nearness to him in time; and it is difficult to understand why Hopkins chose for particular praise certain of the lines mentioned in these letters. There is, rightly and often, a quality to be found in the work of a contemporary that appeals more to the immediate audience than to any other.

Introduction

Bridges has something to say of this when talking of Morris's first and 'absurdly incompetent' poem, which nevertheless was taken seriously by the Brotherhood: 'it follows that there is something in the poem, though we cannot now see it, which at that moment of time was original and remarkable.' Dixon's poems are far from incompetent, but some virtue that appealed with particular force to a former generation is less obvious now. Or so it seems to me. After reading all his verse with care my feeling is that I know Dixon the man, as revealed by Bridges and these letters, far better than Dixon the poet. The poet is difficult to come to grips with, partly no doubt because his manner is mainly 'objective'. His work, miscellaneous in character, seems to lack fixity of purpose, orderly development, and confident concentration. He writes too easily and without waiting for the ripe moment. The admirable qualities of Dixon the man are insufficiently represented in his verses. It is as though he were writing with a veil between himself and life. Perhaps the word 'muffled' will do as well as any to mark this baffling quality.

It is best to approach him, as far as possible, chronologically. *Christ's Company and other Poems* (1861), far too long for a first book, takes its name from the five poems at the beginning that deal with apostles and others who enter Christ's story. At first glance it seems to be a derivative book, with a good deal of ineffective or half-realized work that might well have been excluded. The influence of Browning and Tennyson is apparent, but the ear is more firmly caught by a resemblance in tone and temper to the early work of Morris published with *The Defence of Guenevere* (1858).[1] It might seem, indeed, that Dixon had tried

---

[1] Here are some of the more obvious affiliations:

School of Tennyson: Waiting; Babylon and Nineveh; The Wanderer.

School of Browning: St. Paul, Part of an Epistle from Gallio, the deputy of Achaia, to his brother Seneca; A Nun's Story—Modern Rome; A Monk's Story; Romance [with something of Tennyson].

School of Morris: St. John [with something of Browning]; St. Peter; St. Mary Magdalene; A Lenten Mystery; Dawning; Love's Consolation; La Faerie or Lovers' World; A Song of Three Maidens.

xviii

to apply the theories and methods of Morris to New Testament themes. Thus in *St. Mary Magdalene* we have a crude Pre-Raphaelite picture of a romanticized and medievalized Mary that might almost belong to Morris at his worst:

> Kneeling before the altar step,
> Her white face stretched above her hands;
> In one great line her body thin
> Rose robed right upwards to her chin;
> Her hair rebelled in golden bands,
> And filled her hands;

His figure of Christ's mother, at once too ornate and artful-simple, makes one sigh for *The Dream of the Rood*, and his Peter, over-curious in botany, is a failure. In this group his more ambitious poem on St. John, though unequal and indebted to *Childe Roland to the Dark Tower Came*, is by far the best. There is a good deal of youthful and cloudy picturesque in the vision of horror, but when he comes to describe the Bride of Christ, the vision of saints, and the procession of the seven archangels, an individual rapture takes possession of him. The writing then has a contemplative bloom. These poems no doubt belong to the Oxford days when he shared the happy enthusiasm he has so well described. They are not imitations of Morris. What similarity there may be is due to communion of interest and purpose: the spirit informing them is profoundly different. Dixon, certainly, was unconscious of any debt to Morris, and was not at all pleased to be counted a follower. He writes to Hopkins, on 4 November 1881: 'I do not think I belong to the school of Morris. I have seen very little of his poetry:[1] only three tales of the Earthly Paradise, & a little of Jason. Also that immense work Sigurd. So far as I can judge his touch is entirely different from mine: very powerful, even sledge-hammery: but not over subtle, by no means intellectual, and what I call desolately limited. His creed, that is, his ideas of life, is to me monstrous and insupportable.' Yet without doubting the truth of this, the 'keepings' of the earlier Dixon, one feels, are with Morris and the Pre-

---

[1] This must mean: 'of his later poetry'.

Raphaelites. And this feeling is strengthened by the shorter poems in the book, which, with one exception (the sonnet 'Give me the darkest corner of a cloud'), have no clearly marked individuality. Those that attempt to picture the strange or macabre (such as *The Wizard's Funeral* and *In the Woods*) fall far below their intention. Two other poems stand out by their length. One, *La Faerie or Lovers' World*, another attempt at medieval story, a confused tale of love wherein the ghosts of two lovers commune, is deficient in atmosphere, clarity, and direction. The poet was not possessed by his story and his rhymes often betray him grotesquely. The other poem, *Love's Consolation*, written in heroic couplets, is the most attractive in the book. In it the Monk of Osneyford tells why, after being deceived by his betrothed, he writes tales of love at the bidding of a knight who appears to him in a vision with a small band of unhappy lovers. In plan the poem owes much to the Prologue of Chaucer's *Legend of Good Women*, though there are feeble patches and the story needs more strength. In its love of detail and Chaucerian colour it is essentially a Pre-Raphaelite poem. How excellently simple the descriptive narrative can be the following extracts show. In the first the monk describes the happiness that preluded his disaster.

> It being then the happy Christmas time,
> And all the orchards thick with frosty rime,
> I took me by the happy paths that go
> Along the dumb and frozen river, so
> That I might taste the goodness of the day;
> Passing through many meadows on my way,
> Where all the grass and flowers were dead asleep,
> Through many sheepfolds full of bleating sheep,
> By many watercourses, whereby grew
> The little-headed willows, two and two,
> And also poplars: onward thus I sped,
> Until the pathway reached a little head
> Of brushwood, screening up a wicket gate,
> Whereat I entered, and beheld elate
> A wide and scattered wood of late-leaved beech
> And oaks and thorn-trees, standing on the reach

> Of long-withdrawing glades: at sight of these
> And the snow-dabbled grass, and broken knees
> Of large red ferns in patches, as I went,
> Felt I great exaltation and consent
> Unto the sweetness of the place and day.

The other passage reflects the pain of love.

> The lumpish axe that scales away false skin
> Of some corruption clumped upon the bark,
> Leaves the tree aching with the pale round mark,
> And sweating till the wound be overshot
> By the gums swelling out into a blot,
> Where the bees lose their wings, and dead leaves stick.
> Even so, O love, my flesh was sore and quick
> From that astonishment, when I seemed flayed,
> Torn piecemeal up, and shred abroad, and made
> A victim to some brutal lack of skill.

In this kind of writing, neither bare narrative nor external description, Dixon's strength seems to lie, and one could expect him to develop that side of his talent. He is more at ease when he has a suitable story to tell than when he is attempting lyric measures.

Before coming to his next book mention must be made of *St. John in Patmos*, the Prize Poem on a Sacred Subject for 1863, which was no doubt intended as an addition to *Christ's Company*. The subject is so much to his liking that the verse escapes the usual faults of prize poems and has, indeed, the merits of power and economy of means. The mind behind the writing is immediately attractive; there is something of Dixon himself in this saint who is chosen in his sadness to be blessed:

> For they are ever honoured most who lean
> To human wants from out that cloud serene
> Of solemn thought, in which they fain would dwell,
> But that the world hath need of them to quell
> Its anarchies: they who with burning heart
> Come down their own strong essence to impart,
> And labour noblest things to keep alive:
> True men of action, though contemplative.

His next book, *Historical Odes and Other Poems* (1864), is in most ways disappointing. The critic who spoke of its 'powerful

xxi

dullness' came near the truth. Dixon writes of Marlborough and Wellington as two great heroes of his country and makes a brave attempt to tell their story in verse. The patriotic note is strongly stressed; but the effort is misdirected and reads like the task work it no doubt was, for we are informed that it was part of a design to be executed in collaboration with a friend. The saga of Sir John Franklin, told in heroic couplets and tasting of prize-poem, has little to commend it save a noble ending, and *Havelock's March* is chiefly remarkable for a maddening refrain. Of small consequence also are three poems that form a supplement to *Christ's Company*, and two long narrative poems, competent in the telling but little more, elaborate tales of unhappy love, a theme peculiarly dear to Dixon. Two rehandlings of classical legend, which seem to have their beginnings in *Lamia*, are pleasant to read but have no distinction. Beyond this there are a few odes, sonnets, and lyrics. The ode is a form that Dixon is to use increasingly. Here, for the most part, with Keats and Wordsworth in mind, he seems to be feeling his way, yet the work is more authentic and the touch more assured than in most of the verse in this book. There are noteworthy sections in all four odes, particularly in that *On Departing Youth*, one of Dixon's best shorter pieces, but no inevitability in progression of thought or certainty of shape. Perhaps the ode entitled *To Summer* should be excepted. Both Bridges and Hopkins praise this poem very highly and to differ from such authority is dangerous. Yet it seems to me good without being very good, a distinguished exercise that sends the mind back again and again to the opulent rightness of the *Ode to Autumn* without insisting on a prevailing excellence of its own. Neither in form nor in idiom has it the air of pre-ordained certainty. It wants, too, the sensuous intensity and rich imagery the season seems to demand. This stanza, the third and last, gives a fair idea of its quality:

> Yet thou must fade, sweet nurse of budded boughs;
>   Thy beauty hath the tenderness of death;
> Thy fickle sun is riding from thine house;
>   Thy perfect fulness waits for withering breath:

Already, see, the broad-leaved sycamore
Drops one by one his honours to the floor:
　　For his wide mouths thou canst no longer find,
　Poor mother that thou art, the needful food;
　　The air doth less abound with nectar kind;
　And soon his brethren of the prosperous wood
　Shall paler grow; thou shalt be sallow-hued,
　　　Mother, too soon; dies too
　　　The aspiration thou hast sent,
　　　The thrilling joy, the sweet content
That live with trees so green and heavens so blue.

In the sonnets here Dixon is not markedly successful, principally
because he tends to avoid the discipline of the form by choosing
the easiest of rhyme schemes. The lyrics disappointingly fall
short, all but one, the well-known *Song*, 'The Feathers of the
Willow', that distils the pathos of autumn into two short
stanzas, a poem complete and perfect in its kind.

The volume of 1864, therefore, seems to want a presiding impulse and purpose. Here is verse of many kinds and much evidence of talent, but the author is uncertain of what he wants to
do. Probably he wrote too quickly. The lack of concentration
leads to a good deal of waste.

Mano, the next volume of his verse to appear, was not published till 1883, when the poet was fifty. There is thus a gap of
nearly twenty years to be accounted for. Dixon had always
striven 'to use his poetic gift as an entrusted talent', and during
these years of discouragement he continued to write when occasion called him. Much of this work was afterwards destroyed (as
were the 'reams of *Northern Saga*' remembered by Bridges) or still
remains undiscovered, as is the case with many a poem criticized by Hopkins. But enough was eventually published to show
that he had by him, when he came to know Hopkins and Bridges,
a considerable body of verse. These precious friendships quick-
ened by their praise the flagging impulse to write, and Bridges
records that 'some of his best later pieces seem to have been
composed' between 1879 (the date of his own first visit to
Hayton) and 1881. The same authority tells us that very little

of his verse can be dated as begun after the latter year: 'the lists of 1881 contain almost all the known poems, and show also how many were held back and eventually destroyed.' History thereafter must have absorbed most of his leisure. It is well then to remember that the books printed later by Daniel were composed many years previously. Some of the poems may have been for twenty years in manuscript.

Mano,[1] therefore, did not stand alone, nor was its composition easy. It was written by the poet against the east wind of indifference to fulfil a duty towards himself. Bridges tells the story, but unfortunately he cannot say how long Dixon devoted to the poem, or when be finished it:

'Fearing that the isolation of his clerical routine at Hayton was weaning him from the effort of composition, he determined to bind himself to write at least one canto of this epic every month and bring it with him to the monthly clerical meeting to deposit with a brother parson, whose confidence and sympathy were assured. He punctually executed his task—I cannot say over how long a time it extended—and on the day when he brought the final canto he then for the first time ventured to inquire of his friend what opinion he had formed of the poem. He found that his friend had never had the curiosity to read a line of it.'

The poem does not read like task work. For me it is Dixon's highest achievement and one of the most remarkable narrative poems of the nineteenth century. There are narrative poems that merely add to the telling of a story what charm there may be in accomplished verse. *Mano* is not of their number. The work has in it a core of learning, sympathetic understanding, and living interest. It so happened that Dixon could create for himself a tenth-century world in which it is possible for his readers

---

[1] The full title is: Mano, a Poetical History: of the time of the close of the Tenth Century: concerning the Adventures of a Norman Knight: which fell part in Normandy part in Italy. The poem is dedicated to Bridges. It is written throughout in *terza rima*, a difficult metre handled for the most part in a masterly manner. Dixon intended to follow Italian, rather than English, practice; he attempted to observe Dante's law
>   That round the stanza still the structure play,
>   At end arrested somewhat.

Introduction

to believe, move, and have their being. Whether he is always historically accurate is not the question. His world holds together and is imaginatively shaped. He makes no concession to the manners and morals of his own day; he passes no modern judgements and never prettifies. The main success, therefore, is that most difficult one of atmosphere. The absurdities of Tennyson's *Idylls of the King* and the neverendingness of Morris's later poems are alike avoided. *Mano* is a poem written from a medieval point of view. If it deals with a Middle Ages of convention then that qualification can be given to it only in the sense that Claudel applies it to the world of *L'Annonce Faite à Marie*. There is in it a deeper understanding of things medieval than in Morris's Froissart poems or in those poems by Browning that influenced Morris. The imaginative comprehension of a poet is at work. Dixon lived this poem far more fully than most of his others. It has a life of its own. Perhaps that is what Hopkins refers to when he speaks, on re-reading, of its 'humanity'. In the person of the narrator, the old monk Fergant, there is something of Dixon himself and his charity. There are times, certainly, when history encroaches to the detriment of poetry; and the elaborate intricacy of *Mano's* origin and story is not always warranted. But, as a whole, Dixon the poet is excellently served here by Dixon the historian.

It is impossible to give a brief analysis of *Mano*, nor would an extract or two help much to a knowledge of its quality, for the poem is singularly level and the effect cumulative.[1] It is important, too, not only for what it says, but for what it does not say: its economy of means. But the poem's scope may be suggested. The scheme of it arose from Dixon's reading of the

[1] The following episodes give a fair idea of Dixon's power: The Peasant's Story (medieval necromancy and evil), I. x–xiii; Gerbert and Joanna (adventurous narrative), I. xvi; The Lark's Song, I. xvii; Prodigies and Portents, II. ii; Concerning Vilgardus (rather out of proportion), II. vii; A Monk's Vision of Hell, II. xii; Mano avenges the daughter of Laurentius, and so falls foul of Gerbert, III. v; Fergant's foreshadowing dream, IV. ii; Mano in disguise sees Blanche again, IV. iii; The mind of man, IV. vi; Diantha and Peasants in the wood, IV. vii; The Death of Mano and Joanna, IV. xv.

chronicles round about the year 1000, a time when 'dreadful expectation hung in air' that the world should cease, and writers whose

> thin words drop portents, like a vein
> Too weak to hold the blood

tell of prodigies, tumult, famine, and pestilence. Such writings form a background to the story unfolded by Fergant, now full of age, wisdom, and sorrow, once the disciple of Gerbert the Pope and friend of Mano whose interwoven stories he now tells, to vindicate their glory and set down the truth. The figure of Gerbert, a strange compound of religion, power, and superstition, is Browning's Paracelsus in little, but more firmly imagined and without sentimentality. He it is who ultimately involves Mano, the knight of mysterious origin against whom the stars fight, once his friendly instrument, in disaster; Mano who loves Blanche, betrothed to another, and only after much tribulation in chivalry arrives at the knowledge of his love for her sister Joanna (who has always loved him) at a time when death at once shameful and noble claims them both. These, with the wanton Diantha whose lust for an outlawed peasant leads to an episode comparable to that of Hellenore and the satyrs, are the main figures in the poem. They do not make its sum. A score of minor characters emerge vividly from the narrative. But Dixon's main triumph is in his whole picture of an age whose disorder, superstition, cruelty, and courage is fixed in many an episode remarkable for strokes of bitter irony and unforced pathos, free from virtuous comment. He never exhausts his subject and is admirably detached.

It was this detachment, this absence of a moral other than the purpose of Fergant to set down the truth, that puzzled two of Dixon's sympathetic readers. Hopkins could find no clue to the purpose of the poem; Patmore could not discover 'the inner motive'. There is, of course, reason for such bewilderment. Dixon partly answered the objection when he said there should be found in the poem 'a central motive in faith (in its human aspect fidelity) struggling with fate or accident & misunder-

standing'. He feared that was not made apparent enough.
Certainly it is present in the story of Mano and Joanna. Rightly
he does not underline this one aspect of the poem. Even Mano,
to Hopkins's dismay, is not complete in virtue. Dixon's justi-
fication may perhaps be stated in the words he puts into the
mouth of the heretic Vilgardus, surnamed Grammaticus. Moral
virtue is in her conclusion justified, but:

> Let her alone; be it her part to guide
> To her own mark the capable and strong:
> Nor let Religion touch her proper pride.
> The arts, and all Apollo's learned throng
> Teach life to man; and their own use they have:
> But they accept unhappiness and wrong
> The half of their domain: without the grave
> And mournful part of life what were they all?
> 'Tis theirs to paint, not punish: show, not save.

Mano is the poem of Dixon to which the epithet 'muffled' can
least be applied, but that quality is again present in the three
short volumes, printed by Henry Daniel for limited circulation,
that (save for posthumous publications) complete the tale of his
poetry. Most of the poems were probably written before 1881,
and it is difficult to date more than one or two with certainty.
Dixon explains the decision to seek a private press in a letter to
Hopkins of 14 April 1884: 'The London public have given up
reading poetry. In fact this is not a literary age: & there seems
to be a sort of feeling to retire on Oxford & strive to win the
young.' How far an attempt so forlorn was successful is not yet
clear, for the influence of Daniel's attractive press has yet to be
measured.

Odes and Eclogues (1884), a book of much quiet meditative
beauty, is well represented in Bridges's selection. *Cephalus and
Procris* and *Polyphemus* are true eclogues rich in imagery, lim-
pidly told in heroic couplets with such delicate freshness as to
bring out the pity of their story. Beautiful too is the first stanza
of *The Fall of the Leaf*; but the most characteristic poem in the
book is the irregular *Ode on Conflicting Claims*, which, while lack-
ing Patmore's intensity, seems to owe something to him, and

even suggests, in a turn of thought here and there, the influence of Hopkins. The second stanza discovers the poet's excellence, and shows too, in such phrases as 'quaff the bowl divine', his failure to achieve an altogether personal idiom:

> Thou thinkest that if none in all the rout
> Who compass thee about
> Turn full their soul to that which thou desirest,
> Nor seek to gain thy goal,
> Beauty, the heart of beauty,
> The sweetness, yea, the thoughtful sweetness,
> The one right way in each, the best,
> Which satisfies the soul,
> The firmness lost in softness, the touch of typical meetness,
> Which lets the soul have rest;
> Those things to which thyself aspirest:—
> That they, though born to quaff the bowl divine,
> As thou art, yield to the strict law of duty;
> And thou from them must thine example take,
> Leave the amaranthine vine,
> And the prized joy forsake.

Less satisfactory, to me, is *Lyrical Poems* (1887). Dixon is not primarily a lyric poet; he asks a wider canvas. The shorter pieces in this book, with one or two exceptions, want the virtues of depth and inevitability associated with the lyric form, and their failure to 'explode' (to use a phrase of Hopkins) leaves the reader unsatisfied. Of the two odes that *On Advancing Age*, despite its mood of mellow retrospection, misses the alchemist's touch. The poet is better served by the tired loveliness of his invocation *The Spirit Wooed*, which contains one of those particularly felicitous images that come to him now and again:

> let thy footsteps pass
> Where the river cuts with his blue scythe the grass.

Through the book runs a concern for the nobility of man's endeavour and for the pains of mortality; and this note of regret for the encroachment of age is perhaps most poignantly rendered in *A Country Place Revisited*. One poem, *The Storm Demon*, rather

Introduction

out of key with the rest and not chosen by Bridges, deserves quotation because it anticipates in part the accent of a present-day poet:

> The rock was black, the cloud was white:
>   The black rock in a gorge was set.
> Earth rose, heaven stooped: upon that hight
>   The thunder with the torrent met.
>
> The vast half-weeping cloud came down,
>   Storm-laden: and a demon form,
> Of gathered wrath, stood with a frown
>   Upon that pedestal of storm.
>
> He stood, his rolling mantle spread,
>   His hat of darkness deeply set:
> His locks heaved cloudlike round his head;
>   The torrent lashed his feet of jet.
>
> Forth from his eyes the lightning leapt,
>   His voice spoke with the thunder's tone:
> Earth's waters in swift flashes swept,
>   Her caverns answered with a groan.

Not much can be said for *The Story of Eudocia and her Brothers* (1888), a dull and badly constructed narrative of the saintly Christian Eudocia, who, blameless, is banished by her husband the emperor Theodosius and forgiven too late. Without more intensity in Eudocia herself the poem is pointless. At times there is an approach to the atmosphere found in some of the early lives of saints, but it is only a glimmer. More interesting is the preface, which deals with the measure chosen, one often used by Dixon. His judgement is: 'To write original serious narrative in couplets is the most difficult thing in English versification. . . . As it is the most difficult, so it is the least elevated vehicle for narrative poetry that we possess.'

Last Poems (1905), despite Mary Coleridge's enthusiastic Introduction, falls short of being a worthy memorial volume. There is in it work that Dixon himself would have hesitated to publish. What it contains of value is reprinted in the much more important section, *Posthumous Poems*, of Bridges's selection (1909). Here may be found *Ruffling Wind* and *O Ubi? Nusquam*, two lyrics that rank with Dixon's best; a deeply moving hymn of penitence to God; and two sonnets, *To Hope* and *To Peace*, his most distinguished work in this kind, that attest the beauty of his spirit. Their deliberate retarded movement is peculiarly appropriate to the subtle, long-pondered thought. As will be seen from *To Peace*, it is as though the example of Gerard Hopkins had encouraged him towards the concentration that leads to weightier utterance and a more difficult music:

> O Peace, O Dove, O shape of the Holy Ghost,
>   I would not vex thee with too subtle thought,
> Put thee in fear by hopes, send thee to coast
>   Regions unknown for what I dearest sought.
> To rough delights I would not open course,
>   Nor thy composure fray with vague desire,
> Nor aspiration hold that did thee force,
>   Nor move a step that I could not retire.
>
> Nay, nay, I pray thee, close thy startled eye,
>   Compose again thy self-stirred plumes, nor aim
> At other station, in timidity
>   Of fancied plots, which here I all disclaim.
> Well, fly then! for perchance from heavenward flight
> Gentler on me thou mayst again alight.

The man praised by Rossetti, Swinburne, Bridges, and Hopkins has some claim to be called a poet's poet, yet Dixon's appeal has always been severely small. Bridges, his greatest champion, attempted with little success, in 1896, to win him an audience with a selection called *Songs and Odes* printed in Elkin Mathews's *Shilling Garland*; and though his later selection was received with more favour, Dixon's verse is still not widely known. Not only are all his books of verse (except those issued by Daniel) in print; the original sheets are even yet not exhausted. Last year was the centenary of his birth, but, so far as I know, neither critic nor historian paid him honour. Perhaps the publication of these letters, a belated tribute, may help to a fuller understanding of his mind and thought, and lead many to the rediscovery of his poems. There is some reason for the general lack of response. I cannot agree with Mary Coleridge's dictum that 'the first feeling of nine readers out of ten will be *disappointment*; the second will be *surprise*, the third *ecstasy*'. Dixon rarely spoke out. *Mano* apart, the man is greater than his verses. Yet with a far slenderer natural equipment as poet than Gerard Hopkins possessed, he strove heroically to use the talent entrusted to him to the full. How conscious he was of any fall from the possible best may be seen in his remarks on Tennyson and Carlyle. His gentleness and humility are the reverse of weakness. Behind them lies the fastidious strength that comes from devotion to a great cause.

I

Stonyhurst College, Blackburn. June 4 1878.

Very Rev. Sir,—I take a liberty as a stranger in addressing you, nevertheless I did once have some slight acquaintance with you. You will not remember me but you will remember taking a mastership for some months at Highgate School, the Cholmondeley School, where I then was.[1] When you went away you gave, as I recollect, a copy of your book *Christ's Company*[2] to one of the masters, a Mr. Law[3] if I am not mistaken. By this means coming to know its name I was curious to read it, which when I went to Oxford I did. At first I was surprised at it, then pleased, at last I became so fond of it that I made it, so far as that could be, a part of my own mind. I got your other volume[4] and your little Prize Essay too.[5] I introduced your poems to my friends and, if they did not share my own enthusiasm, made them at all events admire. And to shew you how greatly I prized them, when I entered my present state of life, in which I knew I could have no books of my own and was unlikely to meet with your works in the libraries I should have access to, I copied out *St. Paul, St. John, Love's Consolation,* and others from both volumes and keep them by me.[6]

What I am saying now I might, it is true, have written any time these many years back, but partly I hesitated, partly I was not sure you were yet living; lately however I saw in the *Athenaeum*[7] a review of your historical work newly published

[1] R. W. D. was appointed an assistant master in 1861. There is no record at Highgate of the exact date of his appointment or leaving, but he only stayed a few months. See p. 10.

[2] Published in 1861.

[3] Presumably a mistake for 'Lobb'. See p. 4.

[4] *Historical Odes and Other Poems* (1864). *St. John in Patmos,* the Prize Poem on a Sacred Subject, had been published in 1863.

[5] *The Close of the Tenth Century of the Christian Era*: the Arnold Prize Essay for 1858. [6] See Appendix IV.

[7] A review of *The History of the Church of England from the Abolition of the Roman Jurisdiction*, vol. i, in the issue of 9 February 1878. See NOTE A. The book is also noticed in the *Academy* of 16 February.

and since have made up my mind to write to you—which, to
be sure, is an impertinence if you like to think it so, but I seemed
to owe you something or a great deal, and then I knew what
I should feel myself in your position—if I had written and
published works the extreme beauty of which the author himself the most keenly feels and they had fallen out of sight at
once and been (you will not mind my saying it, as it is, I suppose, plainly true) almost wholly unknown; then, I say, I
should feel a certain comfort to be told they had been deeply
appreciated by some one person, a stranger, at all events and
had not been published quite in vain. Many beautiful works
have been almost unknown and then have gained fame at last,
as Mr. Wells' poem of *Joseph*,[1] which is said to be very fine, and
his friend Keats' own, but many more must have been lost sight
of altogether. I do not know of course whether your books are
going to have a revival, it seems not likely, but not for want of
deserving. It is not that I think a man is really the less happy
because he has missed the renown which was his due, but still
when this happens it is an evil in itself and a thing which ought
not to be and that I deplore, for the good work's sake rather
than the author's.

Your poems had a medieval colouring like Wm. Morris's and
the Rossetti's and others but none seemed to me to have it so
unaffectedly. I thought the tenderness of *Love's Consolation* no
one living could surpass nor the richness of colouring in the
'wolfsbane' and other passages[2] (it is a mistake, I think, and
you meant henbane) in that and *Mark and Rosalys*[3] nor the bright-
ness of the appleorchard landscape in *Mother and Daughter*.[4]
And the Tale of Dauphiny[5] and 'It is the time to tell of fatal

---

[1] *Joseph and his Brethren*, a 'Scriptural Drama', was first published in 1824
under the pseudonym of H. L. Howard. It was reprinted in 1876: Joseph
and his Brethren: / A Dramatic Poem. / By / Charles Wells. / With an introduction by / Algernon Charles Swinburne.

[2] *C.C.*, part of pp. 90–1 (*S.P.*, pp. 34–6).

[3] *C.C.*, *La Faerie, or Lovers' World*, a poem in 62 seven-line stanzas.

[4] *C.C.*, pp. 134–6.

[5] *H.O.*, *Concealment: the Story of a Gentleman of Dauphiny*, pp. 121–30.

love'¹ (I forget the title) in the other book are purer in style,
as it seems to me, and quite as fine in colouring and drawing
as Morris' stories in the *Paradise*, so far as I have read them, fine
as those are. And if I were making up a book of English poetry
I should put your ode to Summer² next to Keats' on Autumn
and the Nightingale and Grecian Urn. I do not think anywhere
two stanzas so crowded with the pathos of nature and landscape could be found (except perhaps there are some in Wordsworth) as the little song of the Feathers of the Willow:³ a tune
to it came to me quite naturally. The extreme delight I felt
when I read the line 'Her eyes like lilies shaken by the bees'⁴
was more than any single line in poetry ever gave me and now
that I am older I could not be so strongly moved by it if I were
to read it for the first time. I have said all this, and could if
there were any use say more, as a sort of duty of charity to make
up, so far as one voice can do, for the disappointment you must,
at least at times, I think, have felt over your rich and exquisite
work almost thrown away. You will therefore feel no offence
though you may surprise at my writing.

I am, Very Rev. Sir, your obedient servant

GERARD M. HOPKINS S.J.

(I am, you see, in 'Christ's Company').

I A

Hayton Vicarage, Carlisle. 8 June 1878.

REVEREND AND MOST DEAR SIR,—I received your Letter two
days ago, but have been unable to answer it before, chiefly
through the many and various emotions which it has awakened
within me. It is probable that I shall not be able to finish this
letter of answer tonight, & that you will receive it at a later date
than might be expected from the date which you read at the top.

¹ *H.O.*, *Perversity: the Story of Ermolai*, pp. 131–43.
² *H.O.*, *To Summer*, pp. 106–7. (*S.P.*, pp. 67–9.)
³ *H.O.*, *Song* (the last poem). (*S.P.*, p. 74.)
⁴ *C.C.*, *St. John*, the first line of stanza xxx.

You cannot but know that I must be deeply moved, nay shaken to the very centre, by such a letter as that which you have sent me: for which I thank you from my inmost heart. I place and value it among my best possessions. I can in truth hardly realise that what I have written, which has been generally, almost universally, neglected, should have been so much valued and treasured. This is more than fame: and I may truly say that when I read your Letter, and whenever I take it out of my pocket to look at it, I feel that I prefer to have been so known & prized by one, than to have had the ordinary appreciation of many. I was talking to my friend Burne Jones the painter[1] a while ago, about three weeks: who said among other things, 'One only works in reality for the one man who may rise to understand one, it may be ages hence'. I am happy in being understood in my life-time. To think that you have revolved my words, so as to make them part of yourself, and have actually copied out some of them, being denied books, is to me indescribably affecting.

I think that I remember you in the Highgate School. At least I remember a pale young boy, very light and active, with a very meditative & intellectual face, whose name, if I am not vastly mistaken, was yours. If I am not deceived by memory, that boy got a prize for English poetry. I may be deceived in this identification: but, if you have time to write again, I should like to know. I little thought that my gift to Mr. Lobb,[2] which I had quite forgotten, would bear such fruit.

With what you say about mifsing fame, I cordially agree. It is often a disadvantage to rise into fame, at least immediate fame; it leads a man to try to excell himself, or strike out something new incefsantly, or at least not to work so naturally and easily as he would if he did not know that the world was watching to see what he will do next.

[1] R. W. D. and Edward Coley Burne-Jones (1838–98) were schoolfellows at King Edward's School, Birmingham, and continued to be friends at Oxford. See *Memorials of Edward Burne-Jones*, by G B-J, 1904, for R. W. D.'s memories of his friend, which reveal a good deal of himself.

[2] Samuel Lobb (Trinity College, Cambridge, 21st Wrangler) was an assistant master at Highgate from 1857–62.

I may just add that I received a letter of warm & high approbation & criticism from Rossetti (whom you mention in your letter) about three years ago, when he read my poems, which he had not seen before.[1] Beside that letter I place yours.

But I am ashamed of writing so much of myself: none is so conscious of my defects as I am. Let me rather regard with admiration the arduous and self-denying career which is modestly indicated in your Letter & signature: and which places you so much higher in 'Christ's Company' than I am.

Believe me yours, with every sentiment of gratitude and esteem

R. W. DIXON.

II

Stonyhurst, Blackburn. June 13 1878.

VERY REVEREND AND DEAR SIR, PAX CHRISTI,—I am very glad now to think I followed my impulse and wrote to you, since my writing could affect you so much and draw out so kind an answer.

I suppose it is me that you remember at Highgate: I did get a prize for an English poem, I do not well remember when; it may have been while you were there.[2] In those days I knew poor Philip Worsley the poet;[3] he had been at school at High-

---

[1] In the advertisements at the end of vol. ii of R. W. D.'s *Church History* is quoted this part of an undated letter from Rossetti: 'By what inexcusable accident I never read them before [*C.C.* and *H.O.*] I cannot now tell; but there is only one impression possible now on doing so, viz., that you are one of the most subtle as well as varied of our poets, and that the neglect of such work as yours on all hands is an incomprehensible accident.' This seems to be the letter mentioned above.

[2] *The Escorial* (Easter 1860) is the only known prize poem written by Hopkins. *The Vision of the Mermaids* was at one time considered to be another. It is now thought that it was not a prize composition.

[3] Philip Stanhope Worsley (1835–66) entered Highgate School in January 1851. He was in the cricket XI of 1853, and won the Governor's Gold Medal for Classics in that year and the next. He was a Scholar of Corpus Christi College, Oxford, and took the Newdigate in 1857 with *The Temple of Janus*. He is perhaps best known for his translation of the *Odyssey* and part of the

gate himself; and spent some time at Elgin House (I suppose as Dr. Dyne's[1] guest) when I was a boarder there; indeed he read over and made criticisms on my successful poem: I recollect that he knew you (perhaps you may have made the acquaintance then, but all these facts I recall detachedly, and cannot group them) and said you would praise Keats by the hour—which might well be: Keats' genius was so astonishing, unequalled at his age and scarcely surpassed at any, that one may surmise whether if he had lived he would not have rivalled Shakspere.

When I spoke of fame I was not thinking of the harm it does to men as artists: it may do them harm, as you say, but so, I think, may the want of it, if 'Fame is the spur that the clear spirit doth raise To shun delights and live laborious days'—a spur very hard to find a substitute for or to do without. But I meant that it is a great danger in itself, as dangerous as wealth every bit, I should think, and as hard to enter the kingdom of heaven with. And even if it does not lead men to break the divine law, yet it gives them 'itching ears' and makes them live on public breath. (You have yourself said something of this— about 'seeking for praise in all the tides of air' in an ode, that 'on Departing Youth', I think[2]) Mr. Coventry Patmore, whose fame again is very deeply below his great merit, seems to have said something very finely about the loss of fame in his lately published odes (*The Hidden Eros*)—I speak from an extract in a review.

What I do regret is the loss of recognition belonging to the work itself. For as to every moral act, being right or wrong,

Iliad into Spenserian stanzas, work praised by Matthew Arnold, among others. See the foreword to the edition of 1875 of his *Poems and Translations* (first published in 1863). He died of consumption.

[1] The Rev. John Bradley Dyne, D.D., Fellow, Dean, and Lecturer in Divinity, Wadham College, Oxford, was appointed Head Master of Highgate in 1838, when the school contained 19 boys. (There were 108 in 1848, and 202 in 1876, two years after Dr. Dyne retired.) The chapel and the older part of the present school were built in his time.

[2] H.O., *Ode on Departing Youth*:

> What has been lost save beating ears
> That sought for praise in all the tides of air, . . .

there belongs, of the nature of things, reward or punishment, so to every form perceived by the mind belongs, of the nature of things, admiration or the reverse. And the world is full of things and events, phenomena of all sorts, that go without notice, go unwitnessed. I think you have felt this, for you say, I remember, in one of the odes: 'What though the white clouds soar Unmarked from the horizon-shore?' or something like that.[1] And if we regret this want of witness in brute nature much more in the things done with lost pains and disappointed hopes by man. But since there is always the risk of it, it is a great error of judgment to have lived for what may fail us. So that if Mr. Burne Jones works for a man who is to arise ages hence he works for what the burning of his pictures or the death of his admirer may for ever cut off. However he in particular has surely many vehement admirers living and even men who have the ear of the public—detractors too no doubt, but who has not? that comes with admiration.

I am happy to think you have an admirer in Mr. Rossetti[2] (Gabriel Rossetti, I suppose): indeed if he read you it could not be otherwise. And I take the same for granted of Mr. Burne Jones.

Let me recommend you, if you have not seen them, my friend Dr. Bridges' poems—not his first little volume of roundels and so forth,[3] now so much the fashion, for I have not read it and

[1] *H.O.*, *Sympathy: An Ode*, pp. 111–14; the passage beginning
> What, if the sea far off
> Do make its endless moan;
> What, if the forest free
> Do wail alone;
> And the white clouds soar
> Untraced in heaven from the horizon shore? . . .

[2] R. W. D.'s 'imperfect recollections' of Rossetti will be found on pp. 36–40 of *Recollections of Dante Gabriel Rossetti*, by T. Hall Caine (1882). They are of great interest, especially in what they say of *The Oxford and Cambridge Magazine*, and of Rossetti as poet, man, and artist, though here R. W. D.'s praise will be held extravagant. These pages help greatly also to an understanding of R. W. D.

[3] *Poems*, 1873: by no means a 'little' book, nor is G. M. H.'s description adequate.

he is ashamed of it and does not wish to be known by it, but a
set of sonnets, a tiny anonymous work no bigger than a short
pamphlet of two dozen pages, they are called *The Growth of
Love* and are to be continued some day. They are strict in form
and affect Miltonic rhythms (which are caviare to the general,
so that his critics, I believe, think him rough) and seem to me,
but I am prepossessed, very beautiful—dignified, both manly
and tender, and with a vein of quaintness. In imagery he is not
rich but excels in phrasing, in sequence of phrase and sequence
of feeling on feeling. Milton is the great master of sequence of
phrase. By sequence of feeling I mean a dramatic quality by
which what goes before seems to necessitate and beget what
comes after, at least after you have heard it it does—your own
poems illustrate it, as 'Yes, one time in the church I think you
mean'[1] or 'It makes me mad' and 'It makes me very sad to think
of all the bitterness he had'.[2] This little work is published by
Pickering[3] and costs only a shilling, I think.

June 15—This letter has run to a greater length than the
little time at my disposal makes justifiable.—It is sad to think
what disappointment must many times over have filled your
heart for the darling children of your mind. Nevertheless fame
whether won or lost is a thing which lies in the award of a
random, reckless, incompetent, and unjust judge, the public,
the multitude. The only just judge, the only just literary critic,
is Christ, who prizes, is proud of, and admires, more than any
man, more than the receiver himself can, the gifts of his own making. And the only real good which fame and another's praise
does is to convey to us, by a channel not at all above suspicion
but from circumstances in this case much less to be suspected
than the channel of our own minds, some token of the judgment
which a perfectly just, heedful, and wise mind, namely Christ's,
passes upon our doings. Now such a token may be conveyed
as well by one as by many. Therefore, believing I was able to

[1] C.C., *La Faerie, or Lovers' World*, st. xxxvi, l. 1.
[2] Ibid., st. xxxi, ll. 3, 6, 7.
[3] A mistake for Bumpus: Pickering published the volume of 1873.

pass a fair judgment as people go, it seemed in the circumstances a charity to tell you what I thought. For disappointment and humiliations embitter the heart and make an aching in the very bones. As far as I am concerned I say with conviction and put it on record again that you have great reason to thank God who has given you so astonishingly clear an inward eye to see what is in visible nature and in the heart such a deep insight into what is earnest, tender, and pathetic in human life and feeling as your poems display.

Believe me, dear sir, very sincerely yours

GERARD HOPKINS S.J.

My address will be after next month 111 Mount Street, Grosvenor Square, London W., where I am to be stationed. But a letter to Stonyhurst would find me.

II A

Hayton Vicarage, Carlisle. 25 Sept. 1878

REVEREND & MOST DEAR SIR,—I feel ashamed when I look at your Letter, to see how long I have left it unanswered: and when I read it again, and consider the just & noble sentiments, the generous kindnefs, and the tender feeling which it breathes, I feel myself doubly criminal. But you must forgive me: for in part I feel personally unworthy to receive the admiration of such a soul as yours: and partly though I have often resolved to write, I have always found myself unequal to it, through emotion or darknefs. I might also plead that I have met with a carriage accident, which laid me up for a long time, after I received your second letter: but this only covers a small part of the time of my silence. I have to thank you from the bottom of my heart for your Letter; for the generous repetition of your opinion that I have been neglected, & your sympathy with the disappointment & pain, which you suppose, not un-justly, that I must have felt: but above all, for the passage in which you point me to Christ as the great critic, the unfailing

9

judge of the gifts which he has given. I have drawn deep consolation from that: it came upon me with the force of a revelation.

You are certainly the same whom I remember as a Boy at Dr. Dyne's: You got the Prize for poetry at the end of the half year that I was there: but, as you seem to remember rightly, you got it after I left, for I had to leave before the end of the half year through illnefs. I remember that we used to dine together in the Boarding House; & that Mr. Lobb and I have often talked of you. He knew more of you than I did: & repeatedly exprefsed his great opinion of your ability. I remember that we once laughed together over some not very laudatory criticism which you passed at table upon 'Father Prout',[1] a facetious writer in the Cornhill Magazine, then newly started. Do you now know anything of Mr. Lobb? As for poor Worsley, I knew him slightly in Oxford, through a man of his College: but I knew nothing of his poetical gifts at the time. I have always regretted that I did not know more of him. My *speaking* acquaintance with him almost begins indeed in Highgate.

I am sorry that I have not yet read the Sonnets of your Friend Dr. Bridges. I have ordered them only to day: for living at some distance from the town, I do not often go in, & when in, I have never happened to remember them before today. I expect great delight from them. I think I know what you mean by 'sequence of phrase' and 'sequence of feeling': and your observations seem to me truly critical: You wish, if I understand aright, to discriminate between them: and to imply that, while Milton was the great master of the one, there are others who excell him in the other: and in fact, the two would hardly be found together. There is in Milton, as I think a sort of absolute precision of language which belongs to no other poet:

---

[1] Francis Sylvester Mahony (1804–66), a Jesuit who, after having been a professor at Clongowes-wood, was expelled from the Order and became a leading contributor to *Fraser's Magazine* as 'Father Prout'. He had some contemporary reputation as a humorist. Before he died, in Paris, he was reconciled to his church. The *Cornhill Magazine* was founded by Thackeray in 1860.

a deliberate unrolling as if of some vast material, which is all there already, and to which the accident of the moment in writing can add nothing: a material which his mighty hands alone can grasp, unroll, & display. If I am at all right, this is what you very happily call 'sequence of phrase'. His matter is more external to himself than in other poets: & at the same time he and his poem make one whole, so that when you think of the one (I mean when you are not reading him) you think of the other also: when you think of the poet, you think of him in relation to his poem. I remember Burne Jones once saying that he thought one line of Milton's the worst that was ever written. It was—'Celestial rosy red, love's proper hue'.[1] He repeated with especial disgust, 'proper hue'. There is certainly something irritating in the verse: but it is perfect in phraseology, if one reflects. One of Milton's qualities was self-sufficiency: which may be said of him both in the best sense, & in a sense not quite the best. It is the quality in his poetry perhaps which gives him 'sequence of phrase'. Of one thing I am certain, that there is a great deal still to be written about Milton. I do not know, for instance, that any critic has done full justice to his *art*.

You speak of Burne Jones:[2] Yes, he has plenty of admirers & wide & spreading fame: and he is an example to your purpose of a man unspoiled by fame: uninfluenced by it in letting it alter his work or his ideal. That is easier for a painter than for a poet: but all honour is due to him for it.

And now, let me ask after yourself: What your pursuit is: Whether you have continued to cultivate the poetic faculty which I must presume to have been given to you: In what is your activity. You will not expect an apology for these questions.

Let me in conclusion recommend to you, if you have not read

[1] *Paradise Lost*, viii. 619.

[2] The opening of the Grosvenor Gallery in 1877 introduced Burne-Jones' work to the general public. The three pictures exhibited (among them was *The Beguiling of Merlin*) met with little hostility, since the doctrines of Ruskin, and the poems of Rossetti and Morris, had prepared the way. R. W. D. dedicated his *Historical Odes* to him.

it, Matthew Arnold's Essay on Maurice de Guérin, the Keats of France, in his 'Efsays in Criticism'.

With much affection, deep interest & gratitude,

Believe me to remain,

Dear Sir,

Yours Sincerely,

R. W. DIXON.

III

111 Mount Street, Grosvenor Square, W. Oct. 5 1878.

VERY REVEREND AND DEAR SIR,—A visit to Great Yarmouth and pressure of work have kept me from answering before yr. very kind letter, and my reply will now not be written at once but as I shall find leisure.

I hope, to begin with, you have quite recovered from the effects of your accident. I escaped from such a one with very little hurt not long ago in Wales, but I witnessed a terrible and fatal coach-accident years ago in the Vale of Maentwrog.

I have forgotten not only what I said about 'Fr. Prout' but even that I ever read him. I always understoo'd that he was a very amusing writer. I do remember that I was a very conceited boy.

I have quite lost sight of Mr. Lobb; I do not even know whether he is alive or dead. The truth is I had no love for my schooldays[1] and wished to banish the remembrance of them, even, I am ashamed to say, to the degree of neglecting some people who had been very kind to me. Of Oxford on the other hand I was very fond. I became a Catholic there. But I have not visited it, except once for three quarters of an hour, since I took my degree. We have a church and house there now.

---

[1] There is confirmation of unhappiness during his last year or two at school in a letter to his friend Luxmoore of 7 May 1862. Here he speaks of a 'terrific altercation' with the head master: 'I was driven out of patience and cheeked him wildly, and he blazed into me with his riding-whip.' Later he goes on to describe the punishment that followed 'a worse row than ever'.

Oct. 6—The other day Dr. Bridges told me he had in vain tried to get yr. volumes of poems, for want of knowing the publisher. I promised I wd. enquire of you. Was it not Smith and Elder?[1]

I quite agree with what you write about Milton. His verse as one reads it seems something necessary and eternal (so to me does Purcell's music). As for 'proper hue', *now* it wd. be priggish, but I suppose Milton means *own hue* and they talk of *proper colours* in heraldry; not but what there is a Puritan touch about the line even so. However the word must once have had a different feeling. The Welsh have borrowed it for *pretty*; they talk of birds singing 'properly' and a little Welsh boy to whom I shewed the flowers in a green house exclaimed 'They *are* proper!'—Milton seems now coming to be studied better, and Masson is writing or has written his life at prodigious length.[2] There was an interesting review by Matthew Arnold in one of the Quarterlies of 'a French critic on Milton'—Scherer I think.[3] The same M. Arnold says Milton and Campbell are our two greatest masters of *style*. Milton's art is incomparable, not only in English literature but, I shd. think, almost in any; equal, if not more than equal, to the finest of Greek or Roman. And considering that this is shewn especially in his verse, his rhythm and metrical system, it is amazing that so great a writer as Newman should have fallen into the blunder of comparing the first chorus of the *Agonistes* with the opening of *Thalaba*[4] as instancing the gain in smoothness and correctness of versification made since Milton's time—Milton having been not only ahead of his own time as well as all aftertimes in verse-structure but these particular choruses being his own highwater mark. It is as if you were to compare the Panathenaic frieze and a teaboard and decide in the teaboard's favour.

I have paid a good deal of attention to Milton's versification

---

[1] Smith, Elder & Co., 65 Cornhill, London.

[2] Masson's *Life of Milton*, 1859 [1858]–1880.

[3] *Quarterly Review*, January 1877, pp. 186–204. Reprinted in *Mixed Essays*, 1879.   [4] See NOTE B.

and collected his later rhythms: I did it when I had to lecture on rhetoric some years since. I found his most advanced effects in the *Paradise Regained* and, lyrically, in the *Agonistes*. I have often thought of writing on them, indeed on rhythm in general; I think the subject is little understood.

You ask, do I write verse myself. What I had written I burnt before I became a Jesuit and resolved to write no more, as not belonging to my profession, unless it were by the wish of my superiors; so for seven years I wrote nothing but two or three little presentation pieces which occasion called for. But when in the winter of '75 the Deutschland was wrecked in the mouth of the Thames and five Franciscan nuns, exiles from Germany by the Falck Laws, aboard of her were drowned I was affected by the account and happening to say so to my rector he said that he wished someone would write a poem on the subject. On this hint I set to work and, though my hand was out at first, produced one. I had long had haunting my ear the echo of a new rhythm which now I realised on paper. To speak shortly, it consists in scanning by accents or stresses alone, without any account of the number of syllables, so that a foot may be one strong syllable or it may be many light and one strong. I do not say the idea is altogether new; there are hints of it in music, in nursery rhymes and popular jingles, in the poets themselves, and, since then, I have seen it talked about as a thing possible in critics. Here are instances—'*Díng, dóng, béll*; Pússy's ín the wéll; *Whó pút* her ín? Líttle Jóhnny Thín. *Whó púlled* her óut? Líttle Jóhnny Stóut.' For if each line has three stresses or three feet it follows that some of the feet are of one syllable only. So too '*Óne, twó*, Búckle my shóe' *passim*. In Campbell you have 'Ánd their fléet alóng the *déep próudly* shóne'—'Ít was tén of Ápril *mórn bý* the chíme' etc; in Shakspere 'Whý shd. *thís* désert bé?' corrected wrongly by the editors; in Moore a little melody I cannot quote; etc. But no one has professedly used it and made it the principle throughout, that I know of. Nevertheless to me it appears, I own, to be a better and more natural principle than the ordinary system, much more flexible, and capable of much greater effects. However I had to mark the stresses in blue chalk, and this and my rhymes carried on from one line into another and certain chimes suggested by the Welsh poetry I had been reading (what they call *cynghanedd*) and a great many more oddnesses could not but dismay an editor's eye, so that when I offered it to our magazine the *Month*, though at first they accepted it, after a time they withdrew and dared not print it. After writing this I held myself free to compose, but cannot find it in my conscience to spend time upon it; so I have done little and shall do less. But I wrote a shorter piece on the Eurydice, also in 'sprung rhythm', as I call it, but simpler, shorter, and without marks, and offered the *Month* that too, but they did not like it either. Also I have written some sonnets and a few other little things; some in sprung rhythm, with various other experiments—as 'outriding feet', that is parts of which do not count in the scanning (such as you find in Shakspere's later plays, but as a licence, whereas mine are rather calculated effects); others in the ordinary scanning *counterpointed* (this is counterpoint: '*Hóme to* his móther's hóuse *prívate* retúrned'[1] and '*Bút to vánquish* by wísdom héllish wíles'[2] etc); others, one or two, in common uncounterpointed rhythm. But even the impulse to write is wanting, for I have no thought of publishing.

I should add that Milton is the great standard in the use of counterpoint. In *Paradise Lost* and *Regained*, in the last more freely, it being an advance in his art, he employs counterpoint more or less everywhere, markedly now and then; but the choruses of *Samson Agonistes* are in my judgment counterpointed throughout; that is, each line (or nearly so) has two different coexisting scansions. But when you reach that point the secondary or 'mounted rhythm', which is necessarily a sprung rhythm, overpowers the original or conventional one and then this becomes superfluous and may be got rid of; by taking that last step you reach simple sprung rhythm. Milton must have known this but had reasons for not taking it.

[1] *Paradise Regained*, iv. 639.   [2] Ibid., i. 175.

I read Arnold's *Essays in Criticism* at Oxford and got Maurice de Guérin's Journal in consequence, admired it, but for some reason or other never got far in it. I should be glad to read it now if I had time. But I have no time for more pressing interests. I hear confessions, preach, and so forth; when these are done I have still a good deal of time to myself, but I find I can do very little with it.

There is a certain Dr. Gordon Hake whose poems are praised by W. Rossetti and other critics. I have seen them in nothing but reviews, but two in particular, *the Young Palmist* and *the Old Snakecharmer*, were very striking.[1] They are more like yours than anything else (for instance the *Wizard's Funeral*[2] or the 'Dying Dawning'[3]). You may perhaps know them.

Believe me, dear Sir, very sincerely yours

GERARD HOPKINS.

Oct. 10.

III A

Hayton Vicarage, Carlisle. 10 Jan. 1879.

REVEREND & MOST DEAR SIR,—It is again long before I answer your interesting & important letter: & again I have to plead partly ill health, partly incessant work in extenuation of a fault which I acknowledge. But I will not let the New Year go farther without sending you at least a greeting & warm good wishes. Your remarks on metre, which form the chief part of your Letter seem to me very curious original & valuable: especially what you say regarding Milton's rhythms. I should like extremely to see in print your collection of these, & your contribution to the understanding of his style. I was much. struck with your discovery that his choruses in Samson are 'counterpointed': I should never have discovered this, but am sure that you are right, & that the discovery is extraordinary, & ought to be made known in justice to the reputation of Milton. I have always admired & wondered at those choruses.

---

[1] See NOTE C.   [2] *C.C.*, p. 60 (*S.P.*, pp. 14–15).
[3] *C.C.*, *Dawning*, pp. 75–6 (*S.P.*, pp. 19–20).

You must be gifted with an extraordinarily delicate ear. I have in an uncritical way observed the difference between the versification of Paradise Lost & P. Regained & the Samson, but without making more of it than that there was a difference: though I remember reading a fine essay by Mr. Seeley on Milton, in which this point is made.[1] The two later poems always reminded me of naked rocks. I never heard of anything more ridiculous than comparing the Samson and Thalaba. Southey was, so far as I know him, the writer who had the smallest notion of style & the least knowledge of the secrets of poetry, considering the magnitude of the works which he attempted. I have not seen Mat. Arnold on the matter, but I s^d think Campbell too small a writer to be put after Milton. It seems rather like naming Raphael and a cameo. I should think that there were lots of little writers of Milton's own age who were writers in style, & equal to Campbell in substance; e.g. Marvel, or Vaughan (I think that is his name). I say with you that Milton is the central man of the world for style: not only of England, but of all the world, ancient & modern. If we want to put some one by him, we had better go to Greece.

I fear that Masson's Life of him is second rate, from the little that I have seen of it: a vile imitation of Carlyle in style. An interesting paper, or even book, might be written on Milton & his Critics: of whom there have been three cycles. 1. Those who examined his art by the classical rules: Addison, & perhaps Johnson: who did this important work well so far as it went, but might be augmented with great advantage to literature. 2. Those who were attracted by his splendour, & partly by his political figure: the writers who wrote when Sumner[2] published his long lost treatise on the Christian Religion: Macaulay,[3]

---

[1] *Lectures and Essays* (1870), by J. R. Seeley, includes *Milton's Political Opinions* and *Milton's Poetry* (pp. 87–154).

[2] Charles Richard Sumner, successively bishop of Llandaff and Winchester, published *De Doctrina Christiana* (Latin text, notes, translation) in 1825.

[3] Macaulay's essay (occasioned by the publication above mentioned) appeared in the *Edinburgh Review* of August 1825.

Channing,[1] Mitford:[2] of whom the first was immeasurably the best, & did much to bring Milton up again: but was unable to understand him as a poet. 3. Those who are now at last grasping the essence of Milton: Arnold, Seeley, & perhaps I may add yourself: or rather perhaps the world may some day.

I have had many notions about Milton at different times, but more concerning his constructive art, & his matter than his verse. One is, that he & Lucretius were the greatest writers of their kind in their languages: & each has given a cosmogony in poetry: the one has perfectly exprefsed *Creation*, the other *the Eternity of Matter*, thus exhibiting the opposite theories. The instantaneous leap to perfection of being by Creation, expressed in the one verse, 'In stately dance uprose the forest trees',[3] seems to me something astounding.

Can you send me the poems on the shipwrecks of which you speak? I hope you can, & the sonnets & other pieces that you have written. I sᵈ like to see a piece in 'sprung rhythm'. Is that anything of the sort that Coleridge meant by his distinction between accent & quantity? You no doubt know of his making that distinction, & giving it out as a discovery; saying that Christabel was written in accent, not quantity, or something like that.[4] Coleridge said also, on reading some of Tennyson's early volumes, that Tennyson did not understand versification —a surprising assertion, which seems to have puzzled everybody. The meaning of that utterance must have been that Tennyson's verse is (very often at least) strictly quantitative, each verse having the same number & disposition of syllables as its fellow in the staff. The most remarkable example of this

---

[1] William Ellery Channing, an American theologian: *Remarks on the character and writings of John Milton; occasioned by the publication of his lately discovered Treatise on Christian Doctrine*, 1826.

[2] The Rev. John Mitford wrote a life of Milton, prefixed to an edition of the poems published in 1832.

[3] This line belongs to Dixon. Milton has (*Paradise Lost*, vii. 323–5)

last
Rose as in Dance the stately Trees and spred
Thir branches hung with copious Fruit: . . .

[4] See NOTE D.

is Locksley Hall, which is without a flaw in this respect. I was reading it over the other day, & while it seemed a wonderfully ingenious piece of versification, wonderfully faithful to the rule which the writer had evidently put before him, yet I grew utterly satiate & weary with it, on this very account. It had the effect of being artificial & *light*: most unfit for intense passion, of which indeed there is nothing in it, but only a man making an unpleasant and rather ungentlemanly row. Tennyson is a great outsider.[1]

I am sorry that after two attempts I was still unable to procure Dr. Bridge's Book: which I much desire to see. My publisher is Smith, Elder & Co. If you can give me in your next letter any directions for procuring Dr. Bridge's Book, I shall be truly glad.

Believe me to be, with all good wishes,

Ever yours sincerely

R. W. DIXON.

P.S. You must excuse me for putting on record another recollection of your school days, which has come to me in writing all this about versification. I remember your saying that ending pentameters with words of two syllables as a rule was only authorised by one poet, Ovid: & that you considered yourself entitled to the freedom of Tibullus.

IV

St. Aloysius' Presbytery, St. Giles's, Oxford. March 10 '79.[2]

VERY REVEREND AND DEAR SIR,—I am still at work upon a letter to you begun last month, but I send this to lose no more time in thanking you for the two pieces of music which reached

---

[1] R. W. D.'s remarks on Tennyson, here and later, are particularly interesting in view of what he says in the Oxford reminiscences contributed to J. W. Mackail's *Life of William Morris* (1889), vol. i, especially pp. 44–6. To the 'brotherhood', *Maud* was Tennyson's 'last poem that mattered' (cf. FitzGerald's judgements in his *Letters*, passim).

[2] This letter was begun later than the one that follows, but, as will be seen, R. W. D. received it earlier.

me from town on Friday last. It was a very kind thought to send them. Your musical townsman is, I hope, an admirer. The 'Feathers of the Willow' was, as you know, an especial favourite of mine. The *Fallen Rain*[1] is new to me. It is the most delicate and touching piece of imagination in the world. While on the one hand delighting in this play of imagination a perverse over-perspectiveness of mind nudges me that the rain could never be wooed by the rainbow which only comes into being by its falling nor could witness the wooing when made any more than the quicksilver can look from the out side back into the glass. However it is the imagination of the 'prescientific' child that you here put on.

Mr. Metcalfe's[2] renderings seem (on two hearings) graceful and sympathetic.

You will, I hope, hear from me more at length presently. Believe me your sincere friend

GERARD M. HOPKINS S.J.

V

St. Aloysius' Presbytery, St. Giles's, Oxford. Feb. 27 1879.

VERY REVEREND AND DEAR SIR,—You will see that I have again changed my abode and am returned to my Alma Mater and need not go far to have before my eyes 'the little-headed willows two and two'[3] and that landscape the charm of Oxford, green shouldering grey, which is already abridged and soured and perhaps will soon be put out altogether, the Wytham and Godstow landscape (as I take it to be) of 'Love's Consolation' and 'Waiting'.[4] We have passed here a bitter winter, which indeed still holds out, and Oxford is but its own skeleton in wintertime. March 4. I have parish work to do, am called one way and another, and can find little time to write.

I am glad to hear that Dr. Bridges has sent you his *Growth of*

[1] Posthumously printed: *S.P.*, pp. 148–9.   [2] See p. 91.
[3] *C.C.*, *Love's Consolation*, p. 85, l. 10 (*S.P.*, p. 26, l. 6).
[4] *C.C.*, pp. 101–4.

Love (his last copy) and the new book and that you were pleased with them.

In the new book three poems, the 'Passer By', the 'Downs', and a sonnet beginning 'So hot the noon was' are written in a mitigated sprung rhythm. But to understand a new thing, such as this rhythm is, it is best to see it in an extreme example: you will then rather appreciate their peculiarities from it than that from them. March 7. I cannot just now get at Coleridge's preface to *Christabel*. So far as I can gather from what you say and I seem to have seen elsewhere, he was drawing a distinction between two systems of scanning the one of which is quite opposed to sprung rhythm, the other *is not, but might be developed into*, that. For though it is only a step from many popular and many literary cadences now in being to sprung rhythm and nature even without that help seems to prompt it of itself, yet the step has never, that I know of, been taken. The distinction Coleridge, as I suppose, was drawing (though it is a great abuse of terms and usage to make it by the words Accent and Quantity) is between strictly *counted rhythm*, in which, if iambic e.g., each foot has two syllables only and is an iamb; if anapaestic, each foot has three syllables and is an anapaest—this on the one hand, and, on the other, mixed rhythm, in which feet of the same kind maybe used interchangeably, as iambs with anapaests, because both belong to *rising rhythm*, or trochees with dactyls, because both belong to *falling rhythm*. And this mixture maybe of two sorts—*equal-timed*, as in the hexameter, where the spondee is used as the alternative of the dactyl, because it is of equal length; or *logaoedic*, as when in classical and therefore strictly timed metres dactyls are mixed with trochees, which feet are of unequal length. (I leave out here all consideration of the still freer mixed lyric rhythms of antiquity.) However this last division is of little importance or meaning in English verse. It is enough that we can interchange two-syllabled with three-syllabled feet. This is freely done in ballad-measures and Coleridge does it in *Christabel*. In the more stately metres the poets of the last century as well as others before and since employ only the stricter counted rhythm,* but even in the fivefoot iambic Tennyson and other modern poets often make two light syllables count for one.

This practice is founded upon an easily felt principle of *equal strengths*, as in the classic hexameter the substitution of spondees for dactyls is founded on the principle of equal lengths (or times). To go a little deeper, it supposes not only that, speaking in the abstract, any accent is equal to any other (by accent I mean *the* accent of a word) but further that each accent may be considered to be accompanied by an equal quantity of slack or unaccented utterance, one, two, or more such unaccented syllables; so that wherever there is an accent or stress, there there is also so much unaccentuation, so to speak, or slack, and this will give a foot or rhythmic unit, viz. a stress with its belonging slack. But now if this is so, since there are plenty of accented monosyllables, and those too immediately preceded and followed by the accents of other words, it will come about that a foot may consist of one syllable only and that one syllable has not only the stress of its accent but also the slack which another word wd. throw on one or more additional syllables, though here that may perhaps be latent, as though the slack syllables had been absorbed. What I mean is clearest in an antithesis or parallelism, for there the contrast gives the counterparts equal stress; e.g. 'sanguinary consequences, terrible butchery, frightful slaughter, fell swoop': if these are taken as alternative expressions, then the total strength of *sanguinary* is no more than that of *terrible* or of *frightful* or of *fell* and so on of the substantives too.

Now granting this, if the common ballad measure allows of our having (say) in a fourfoot line 'Terrible butchery, frightful slaughter' why, on principle, shd. we not say 'Terrible butchery, fell swoop' and that be four feet? or further why not 'Sanguinary consequences, terrible butchery'?—except indeed, what of course in practice and actual versewriting is important, that *conse-*

* Even to the absurdities of 'fond mem'ry's voice' and 'th' umbrageous grove'.

quences is a clumsy halting word which makes the line lag. This then is the essence of sprung rhythm: *one stress makes one foot,* no matter how many or few the syllables. But all that I have said is of course shewing you the skeleton or flayed anatomy, you will understand more simply and pleasantly by verses in the flesh.

March 10—You are kind enough to ask to see my poems. You shall do so when I have got the two shipwreck-pieces back, which are not at hand, and have copied the sonnets out fair. But though the number is small I find this no easy matter.

Reading over what I have written above I find it very hurried and confused: I hope you may gather some meaning out of it. I shd. add that the word Sprung which I use for this rhythm means something like *abrupt* and applies by rights only where one stress follows another running, without syllable between. Besides the bare principle which I have been explaining I employ various artifices which you will see in reading.

To turn to your letter—I am not surprised at what Arnold says of Campbell. Cold and dull as the *Pleasures of Hope* is and much more that he wrote, there is always the 'freehand' of a master in his work beyond almost all our poets, and when one turns from his frigidities to what are held his masterpieces and will always keep his name green, the *Battle of the Baltic* and so forth, one finds a kind of inspired felicity seen no where else that he himself could not have analysed or justified. An inversion and a phrase like 'On the deck of fame that died' or the lines 'But the might of England flushed To anticipate the scene' seem to me as if the words had fallen into their places at a magic signal and not by any strain and continuance of thought.

Marvel, of whom I have only read extracts, is a most rich and nervous poet. Thomas[1] Vaughan's poems were reprinted not so long ago.[2] He was a follower of Herbert both in life and style: he was in fact converted from worldly courses by reading Herbert's poems on a sickbed and even his muse underwent a

[1] A slip for 'Henry'.
[2] The edition of the Rev. H. F. Lyte (Pickering, 1847).

23

conversion (for he had written before). He has more glow and
freedom than Herbert but less fragrant sweetness. Somewhere
he speaks of some spot 'primrosed and hung with shade'[1] and
one piece ends

> And here in dust and dirt, O ,here
> The lilies of his love appear.[2]

(I am assuming that you have not got the book.) Still I do
not think him Herbert's equal.

You call Tennyson 'a great outsider'; you mean, I think, to
the soul of poetry. I feel what you mean, though it grieves me
to hear him depreciated, as of late years has often been done.
Come what may he will be one of our greatest poets. To me his
poetry appears 'chryselephantine'; always of precious mental
material and each verse a work of art, no botchy places, not
only so but no half wrought or low-toned ones, no drab, no
brown-holland; but the form, though fine, not the perfect
artist's form, not equal to the material. When the inspiration
is genuine, arising from personal feeling, as in *In Memoriam*,
a divine work, he is at his best, or when he is rhyming pure and
simple imagination, without afterthought, as in the *Lady of
Shalott, Sir Galahad*, the *Dream of Fair Women*, or *Palace of Art*.
But the want of perfect form in the imagination comes damag-
ingly out when he undertakes longer works of fancy, as his Idylls:
they are unreal in motive and incorrect, uncanonical so to
say, in detail and keepings. He shd. have called them *Charades
from the Middle Ages* (dedicated by permission to H. R. H. etc).
The Galahad of one of the later ones is quite a fantastic charade-
playing trumpery Galahad, merely playing the fool over Christian heroism. Each scene is a triumph of language and of
bright picturesque, but just like a charade—where real lace and
good silks and real jewelry are used, because the actors are
private persons and wealthy, but it is acting all the same and
not only so but the make-up has less pretence of correct keeping
than at Drury Lane. His opinions too are not original, often
not independent even, and they sink into vulgarity: not only

[1] *Silex Scintillans, Regeneration*, st. 1, l. 4.   [2] *Thalia Rediviva, The Revival.*

Locksley Hall but *Maud* is an ungentlemanly row and *Aylmer's Field* is an ungentlemanly row and the *Princess* is an ungentlemanly row. To be sure this gives him vogue, popularity, but not that sort of ascendancy Goethe had or even Burns, scoundrel as the first was, not to say the second; but then they spoke out the real human rakishness of their hearts and everybody recognised the really beating, though rascal, vein. And in his rhetorical pieces he is at his worst, as the *Lord of Burleigh* and *Lady Clare Vere de Vere* (downright haberdasher). But for all this he is a glorious poet and all he does is chryselephantine. Though by the by I owe him a grudge for *Queen Mary*, written to please the mob, and for that other drama where a portent of a man in flaxen locks and ring-mail mouths rationalism 'to torment us before the time'.[1]

I remember what I said about Latin elegiacs but I think I was wrong. Ovid carried the elegiac couplet to a perfection beyond which it could not go and his work remains the standard of excellence. He fixed the system of counterpoint for the elegiac couplet, as Horace for the Sapphic and Alcaic stanzas. This is a long intricate matter, to which I have paid some attention but I can write little about it now. It shd. however be said that in the *Fasti* Ovid does now and then employ the three-syllable ending. To shew the advance made in the counterpointing of the elegiac couplet take the following small point. Words with *-que*, *-ne*, *-ve* attached were always accented on the syllable before, whereas when the *-que* etc was part of the word itself (as in *utique*, *itaque* it may be) it followed the usual accentuation. In such a dactyl then as *armaque* the accent of the word would not in elegiac verse agree with the accent of the verse, the stress; which shd. fall on the first syllable. Here at once is counterpoint. Now in the sensitive places of the couplet, the fifth foot of the hexameter and the second half of the pentameter, Propertius never ventures on this counterpointing except once in all his works. Ovid employs and parades it: the first pentameter of the *Fasti* is

Lapsáque sub térras ortáque sígna cánam—

[1] *Harold* (1876).

in which the word-accent only once (in *signa*) agrees with the stress of the rhythm. The accentuation is the same as in English would be

The rísings and séttings of stárs I méan to síng of—

which is nothing like a pentameter.

I have just got back my two wreck-pieces, which with the sonnets I hope to send you in a few days. This letter is longer than I had any business to write.

Believe me your sincere friend

GERARD M. HOPKINS S.J.

March 12 1879.

March 13—I have been up to Godstow this afternoon. I am sorry to say that the aspens that lined the river are everyone felled.[1]

· VI

The Catholic Church, St. Giles's, Oxford. March 29 1879.

VERY REVEREND AND DEAR SIR,—I now send my pieces: please return them when done with, as I have no other copies. It is best to read the *Eurydice* first, which is in plain sprung rhythm and will possess you with the run of it. The *Deutschland*, earlier written, has more variety but less mastery of the rhythm and some of the sonnets are much bolder and more licentious. The two pieces written here at Oxford have not their last finish.

I hope you will like them.

Believe me your sincere friend

GERARD M. HOPKINS S.J.

VI A

Hayton Vicarage, Carlisle. 5 April 1879.

REVEREND AND MOST DEAR SIR—I have your Poems and have read them I cannot say with what delight, astonishment, & admiration. They are among the most extraordinary I ever

[1] *Poems*, 19: 'Binsey Poplars, felled 1879. Oxford, March 1879.'

read & amazingly original. I write to say this, not in answer to your letter, to which I will reply when I can: and say more of the Poems.

It seems to me that they ought to be published. Can I do anything? I have said something of the institution of your Society in my next volume of Church History, which is not yet published.[1] I could very well give an abrupt footnote about your poems, if you thought good. You need not answer about this before you hear from me again, as I shall not be ready for the Prefs for a year. You may think it odd for me to propose to introduce you into the year 1540, but I know how to do it. My object would be to awaken public interest & expectation in your as yet unpublished poems: or your recently published, if you think of publishing before that time.

By the way, I should have told you before that I have no title to be called *Very* Reverend. I have somehow always neglected or forgotten this at the time of writing.

Believe me with the sincerest admiration
Your friend
R. W. DIXON

I have delayed posting this by accident.

VII

St. Aloysius' Clergy House, St. Giles's, Oxford. May 12 1879.

REVEREND AND DEAR SIR,—Let me first apologise for mis-styling you: it is a blunder I ought not to have made, but our Canons are styled Very Reverend, I daresay by a modern usage, and without enquiring to set myself right I followed that example.

I should have written before but that my superior had a carriage-accident (like you not long since), broke his collar-bone, and was at the hardest time of our year laid up in the country, all the work falling on me, and so in great measure it does still after he has returned, for he is laid up with another

---

[1] It was reviewed in the *Academy* of 12 March 1881.

complaint. The work I find very tiring and it leaves me no time for reading and makes letterwriting hard. This is my excuse for not acknowledging your very kind words sooner.

It was of course a very great pleasure to have so high an opinion expressed of my poems and by you.

But for what concerns the notice you kindly offer to make of me in your forthcoming volume, it would not at all suit me. For this there are several reasons, any one sufficient; but it is enough to say now that (1) I have no thought of publishing until all circumstances favour, which I do not know that they ever will, and it seems that one of them shd. be that the suggestion to publish shd. come from one of our own people; (2) to allow such a notice would be on my part a sort of insubordination to or doubledealing with my superiors. But nevertheless I sincerely thank you for your kind willingness to do me a service.

The life I lead is liable to many mortifications but the want of fame as a poet is the least of them. I could wish, I allow, that my pieces could at some time become known but in some spontaneous way, so to speak, and without my forcing.

Believe me, with many thanks for the kindness which your letters always breathe, your sincere friend

GERARD M. HOPKINS S.J.

VII A

Hayton Vicarage, Carlisle. 31 May 1879

REVEREND & MOST DEAR SIR,—I should have answered your Letter before, but that I have been away from home in the South: & only returned the day before yesterday. I am sorry that you cannot see your way to the notice which I proposed of your poems. I did not think that you would allow it without the knowledge of your Superiors, but I thought (in a dim way, for I know little of your obligations) that you might have got their consent, perhaps by shewing them my Letter.

I have not looked at your poems since my return, but I am sure that my first imprefsion is true of their extraordinary merit.

I have been reading Shakespeare's Henry the Eighth, while in the South: the metre is wonderfully free, & like what you indicate in your remarks. I rather think it was one of his later plays.

I will write again in a month or two, when I have thoroughly read your poems again, & return them.

Many thanks for your kind note.

Believe me ever yours most truly

R. W. Dixon

VII B

St. Mary's Vicarage, Hayton, Carlisle. 19 Oct. 1879.

Reverend & Most Dear Sir,—I feel that I have kept your Poems longer than I ought; but I am unwilling to send them back without doing something.

Should you be angry that I sent your Lofs of the Eurydice, or part of it, to one of the Carlisle Papers, giving your name, and a line or two of introduction from myself?

Ever yours

R. W. Dixon

VIII

St. Joseph's, Bedford Leigh, near Manchester. Oct. 24 1879.

Reverend and dear Sir,—I have left Oxford and am appointed to Liverpool (St. Francis Xavier's, Salisbury Street). I am uncertain how long I shall be at Leigh. The place is very gloomy but our people hearty and devoted.

I cannot be quite sure from your words whether you have sent the verses to the paper or only were thinking of sending; I suppose however that they are sent. If it is too late to recall them the matter can not be helped. I am troubled about it because it may come to the knowledge of some of ours and an unpleasant construction be put upon it. It would be easy to explain it to the Provincial, but not so easy to guard myself against what others might say. However we have no house at or near Carlisle, so that I daresay it may pass without notice taken. You, I know, acted out of pure kindness, but publication of my lines except by the ordinary channels cannot serve me. You would not, I hope, think I secretly wished to steal a march upon my superiors: that would be in me a great baseness. I believe after all that no great harm will have been done, since Carlisle papers are not likely to have more than a local circulation; but do not send them any more pieces.

The learned Fr. Joseph Stevenson,[1] who joined our body two years ago very late in life, and his friend the Rev. Mr. Sole, late of Oscot, also an antiquary, by my persuasion made themselves acquainted with the first volume of your history (I have not looked at it myself, I have no time for study, at least at Oxford I had none) and reported to me highly of its learning and spirit. I hope it is going on well.

Believe me affectionately your friend

GERARD M. HOPKINS, S.J.[2]

IX

St. Joseph's, Bedford Leigh. Oct. 31 1879

MY DEAR CANON,—Pray do not send the piece to the paper: I cannot consent to, I forbid its publication. You must see that to publish my manuscript against my expressed wish is a breach of trust. Ask any friend and he will tell you the same.

Moreover this kind of publication is very unlikely to do the good that you hope and very likely to do the harm that I fear. For who ever heard of fame won by publication in a local paper, and of one piece? If everything of its intrinsic goodness gravitated to fame your poems wd. long since have been famous. Were Tennyson, putting aside marks of style by which he might

---

[1] 1806–95: the well-known archivist and editor of numerous texts. He was born a Presbyterian; later took Anglican orders, was received into the Church of Rome in 1863, and, after his wife's death, ordained priest in 1872. When the Public Record Office was instituted, he was one of the first editors engaged. He became a Jesuit in 1877, and still continued his historical research.

[2] R. W. D.'s answer to this letter, in which it seems he again urged publication, is missing.

be recognised, to send something to the *Nineteenth Century* or best circulated London magazine *without his name* it wd. be forgotten in a month: now no name and an unknown name is all one. But what is not near enough for public fame may be more than enough for private notoriety, which is what I dread.

You say truly that our Society fosters literary excellence. Why then it may be left to look to its own interests. It could not approve of unauthorised publication, for all that we publish must be seen by censors first.

Then again if you were to print my piece you would surely not mutilate it. And yet you must; for with what grace could you, a clergyman of the Church of England, stand godfather to some of the stanzas in that poem? And besides I want to alter the last stanza.

Nov. 1—This letter, which the pressure of parish work has delayed, will now, I daresay, be too late and the Eurydice may have appeared. You will see that your warmhearted but much mistaken kindness will be unavailing: if the paper takes the piece (which it is sure to misprint) few will read it and of those few fewer will scan it, much less understand or like it. (To be sure the scanning is plain enough, but people cannot, or they will not, take in anything however plain that departs from what they have been taught and brought up to expect: I know from experience). Indeed I am in hopes that the matter may even escape the notice of our own people.

Believe me affectionately your friend

GERARD M. HOPKINS S.J.[1]

X

St. Joseph's, Bedford Leigh, near Manchester. Nov. 5 1879.

MY DEAR CANON,—I am very glad that all has blown over and no harm done. You are very welcome to shew my poems to anyone you like so long as nothing gets into print.

[1] R. W. D.'s answer, the gist of which can be gathered from the next letter, is missing.

I will, when I can feel that I can spare the time, send you a few more pieces composed since what you have, and you can keep the copies. I am thinking of a tragedy on St. Winefred's Martyrdom[1] and have done a little and of another on Margaret Clitheroe,[2] who suffered by pressing to death at York on Ouse Bridge, Lady Day 1586 (I think): her history is terrible and heartrending.

Have you any thoughts of publishing another volume of poems?

Believe me your affectionate friend

GERARD M. HOPKINS S.J.

X A

S. Mary's Vicarage, Hayton, Carlisle, 1 Mar. 1880

REVEREND AND MOST DEAR SIR,—I return your Poems at last, having copied some, but not so many as I wished. I have so much writing on hand with the second volume of my History, that I have not been able to do all that I would. I have read them many times with the greatest admiration: in the power of forcibly & delicately giving the essence of things in nature, & of carrying one out of one's self with healing, these poems are unmatched. The Eurydice no one could read without the deepest & most ennobling emotion. The Sonnets are all truly wonderful: of them my best favourites are the Starlight Night, the Skylark, Duns Scotus Oxford: and the Windhover.

I am haunted by the lines—

> 'And you were a liar, o blue March day,
> Bright, sunlanced fire of the heavenly bay.'[3]

which seem to me more English-Greek than Milton, or as much so, & with more passion. The Deutschland is enormously powerful: it has however such elements of deep distress in it

---

[1] *Poems*, 36 and 58.   [2] *Poems* (2nd ed.), 86.
[3] *Poems*, 17, *The Loss of the Eurydice*, ll. 21–2 (2nd line misquoted: see p. 33).

that one reads it with lefs excited delight though not with lefs interest than the others. I hope that you will accept the tribute of my deep and intense admiration. You spoke of sending me some more. I cannot in truth say what I think of your work.

Believe me ever your deeply attached friend

R. W. DIXON.

XI

8 Salisbury Street, Liverpool. May 14 1880.

MY DEAR FRIEND,—I write to remove the appearance of neglect in not answering the letter you enclosed with my poems.

I never saw it till yesterday. When the enclosures came I did not open them and it did not occur to me that there might be a letter within. I put them by in a drawer and they might have lain longer, but it happened that I wanted a sizeable envelope to keep something, when to my great joy I came upon what you had written.

I thank you earnestly for the words so deeply kind and cheering in which you express your judgments. In one point I seem to have your admiration on false pretences. What I wrote was

Bright sun lanced fire in the heavenly bay, etc—

that is/ a bright sun was darting fire from the bay of heaven, but that was of no avail, for did not a fatal north wind . . . and so on.

I will send what else I have whenever I can find an opportunity of copying it. The parish work of Liverpool is very wearying to mind and body and leaves me nothing but odds and ends of time. There is merit in it but little Muse, and indeed 26 lines is the whole I have writ[ten][1] in more than half a year, since I left Oxford.

Believe me your affectionate friend

GERARD M. HOPKINS S.J.

May 15.

[1] A hyphen shows that G. M. H. intended this.

Hayton

XI A

S. Mary's Vicarage, Hayton, Carlisle. 22 June 1880

MY DEAR FRIEND,—I have been long in acknowledging your last letter: for which I thank you. If any thing that I have said of your work has given you pleasure, I wish I could double the pleasure by doubling what I said, for it would still be true. I look for the promised residue when you can send it.

This is a hasty line at last: for I am busy with many things: not the least being the paſsage of my 2nd vol. of Ch. Hist. through the preſs. You spoke in favourable terms of it, & of opinion of one or two of your Friends concerning it—I mean the 1st vol. I am very glad to have your good opinion, if of nothing else at least of the spirit in which I try to write. My aim is to get the exact truth, & give that, with whatever colour. I mean, that I do not pretend to be without prepossessions & bias; if I had not those, I should not take the labour of writing at all: but I hope never to be found suppreſsing, telling half a story, concealing anything connected with any point at issue, or otherwise dealing dishonestly with materials. This is what I mean by historical honesty: not the having no bias or side. I need not tell you that some of our best known writers are gravely wanting in this sort of honesty. I may add that I aim at writing a work of importance: not at adding to the pestering swarm of little books with which we are afflicted.

With every good wish I am Your affect^e friend

R. W. DIXON

I wish you had more leisure for writing

XI B

Hayton Vicarage, Carlisle. 15 Nov. 1880.

REVEREND & MOST DEAR SIR,—It seems long since I heard from you, so long that I am not quite sure whether I or you wrote last: but I think that it was I. Since that however I have seen & come to know Bridges,[1] & have heard much of you from

[1] Here should be read pp. xviii–xx of R. B.'s *Memoir* prefixed to *S.P.*

34

him, & seen in his Book of your MSS. some poems that I had
not seen. I can only say that they confirm, not increase, the
admiration which I feel: and which is so great as to convince
me that you must from pure sympathy have much over-rated
my own writings: which are very imperfect in comparison with
yours or his. But I can ill afford to lose your sympathy.

I greatly admire his last ifsue[1] of poems: especially the first
piece 'Indolence'—& two of those in the 'new prosody', viz.
London Sun[2] & the Voice of Nature: the two first lines of the
latter seem to me unsurpassable.[3] The Dead Child I thought
less of at first: but now think exquisite.

This 'new prosody', which is your invention, exercises me
greatly. I think I understand it in a general way from your
poems and written explanations. But the question is whether it
can be laid down or drawn out in a system of rules. Eventually,
in application, I suppose it must be a matter of ear, rather than
of formal rule: but still it has principles that can be expressed,
and therefore might form a system. I asked Bridges whether
the foundation of it did not lie in fixed quantity, and he said
that it did, but that much more was involved in it. This however would in itself involve a revolution; and a great deal of
work, though very valuable work, if certain terminations, e.g.
or certain words also, were decided to be absolutely long or
short. For instance, the word *over* is long in the first syllable, &
generally so used (I owe this to Bridges, I had never thought
about it): but Tennyson uses it short (I think) in the Ode to
Memory.[4]

Have you any thought of drawing it out in a system?[5]

I should like to send you two or three poems to criticise,

---

[1] *Poems,* by the author of *The Growth of Love,* *Third Series.*

[2] Thus in MS.: *London Snow.*

[3]   I stand on the cliff and watch the veiled sun paling
      A silver field afar in the mournful sea.

[4] This seems to be an error. 'Over' is used three times in the *Ode to
Memory*, in sections ii, iv, and v.

[5] Here follows a passage of 4½ lines that is cancelled: it is uncertain by
whom.

if you would care to look over them. If not, do not hesitate to say so.

I have been reading over Tennyson again. I wish he had not palled upon me so much. The fault is, must be, in me: but I read things that I used to admire extremely with the mere remembrance, not revival, of my former feelings. And yet it is not so with Milton or Keats. The Ode to Memory seemed to me very imperfect, the repeated lines (O strengthen me &c) to have little meaning: & the expression & verse to be sometimes imperfect. Fancy talking of the 'coves' of a brook![1]

Believe me

                                        Yours most sincerely

                                                  R. W. Dixon

XII

                      8 Salisbury Street, Liverpool. Dec. 22 1880.

MY DEAR FRIEND,—A letter was already owing from me to you and I had long been meaning to write and had your name on a list before me, when your last, now five weeks old, overtook me in the midst of my lingerings and my hinderings. I began to answer it, but that answer was never finished: perhaps this happened more than once. My parish work has been very wearisome; of late especially; it appeared to me at last that I never should be able to get my letters written. Now I am flattering myself that this big paper helps me on.

I thank you very much for your comforting praises. I cannot see what should make me overrate your poems: I had plenty of poetry old and new to compare with them and to guide my taste, I read them of my own choice years before I ever thought of communicating with you. I did not, it is true, care very much for some of them, such as the Romance beginning 'Rightly be swift',[2] and there are passages in most of them, even in those I value most, which I could not and can not understand, obscurities of expression which are, I think, of themselves and not through the reader's want of apprehension faulty; but

---

[1] Dimple in the dark of rushy coves.
[2] *C.C., Romance*, pp. 144–6. This is the first line of the third stanza.

against these I set their extreme beauties—imagery inheriting
Keats's mantle, the other-world of imagination (constructive
imagination is rare even among poets), the 'instress' of feeling,
and a pathos the deepest, I think, that I have anywhere found.
(By the by there is one thing that Keats's authority can never
excuse, and that is rhyming open vowels to silent *r*s, as *higher*
to *Thalia*: as long as the *r* is pronounced by anybody, and it is
by a good many yet, the feeling that it is there makes this
rhyme most offensive, not indeed to the ear, but to the mind.)
Your second volume I never knew so well as the first nor did
the historic odes themselves interest me so much as the pieces
of Christ's Company, not that they do not mark an advance in
power, but for just the reason that their subjects or motives had
less interest and also perhaps because they were transitional
and you had not altogether made your own some new ground
you seemed moving on to. But pieces like the Ode to Summer
in that volume are in point of art and execution more perfect
than any in the older one.

Bridges of course told me about his visit to you when I saw him
in town in the summer.[1] He spoke of your epic on some legend
of the northern mythology, and praised its beauties, but said
he had pointed out to you that it too much resembled *Hyperion*.
I had thought of asking you to let me see it but held back for
want of time. Now however I shall be only too happy to see
the pieces you offer to send and will, if you wish, make what
remarks may occur to me as opportunity shall serve. I read
some beautiful pieces of yours in his book—the Murder in the
Dark,[2] some sonnets on Man, a reflective Ode on the pleasures

[1] The next two sentences are cancelled in the MS. R. B., however, wrote
them on the cover of this letter, and added, in brackets, the following note:
[R. W. D. had reams of Northern epics. I did not praise them: but praised
'Mano', in the revision of which I worked hard, tho' I c^d not persuade D to
mitigate the historical diversions as much as I wished. But who erased this
passage? Certainly not G. M. H. & it is unlike D to have erased it. I do
not remember erasing it: tho' I may have done so when first the letters came
into my hands, on acc^t of the misrepresentation which it conveys. I think
R. W. D. burned all these Epics. R. B. July 1907.]

[2] Perhaps re-named?

of learning and the sorrows of sympathy[1] (I forget its name), perhaps some other things I cannot now recall. This Ode expresses something of what your letter speaks of in the case of Tennyson, the loss of taste, of relish for what once charmed us. I understand that state of mind well enough; it used at one time to dismay and dishearten me deeply, it made the best of things seem empty. I think that many things contribute to it and play a part. One is a real disenchantment, the correction of the earlier untrained judgment or taste by the maturer one —as, suppose a child thought Macaulay's Lays the finest poetry that ever was penned: I daresay many do. Another is the short-coming of faculty in us, because the enchanting power in the work is finite or because the mind after a certain number of shocks or stimuli, as the physiologists would say, is spent and flags; and this is plainly the case with jokes, however witty and whimsical: you know that they *are* good, you laughed and were right to laugh heartily when you first heard them, but now they are stale to you and you could laugh no more. Another is that insight is more sensitive, in fact is more perfect, earlier in life than later and especially towards elementary impressions: I remember that crimson and pure blues seemed to me spiritual and heavenly sights fit to draw tears once; now I can just see what I once saw, but can hardly dwell on it and should not care to do so. Another is—or it comes to one of the above—the greater demand for perfection in the work, the greater impatience with technical faults. In the particular case of Tennyson's Ode to Memory I find in my own case all these: it has a mysterious stress of feeling, especially in the refrain—I am to my loss less sensitive to that; it has no great meaning of any importance nor power of thought—I am to my advantage more alive to that; from great familiarity with the style I am deadened to its individuality and beauty, which is again my loss; and I perceive the shortcomings of the execution, which is my own advance in critical power. Absolutely speaking, I believe that if I were

---

[1] *Ode on Conflicting Claims*: first published in *Odes and Eclogues*, 1884; *S.P.*, pp. 77–80.

now reading Tennyson for the first time I should form the same judgment of him that I form as things are, but I should not feel, I should lose, I should never have gone through, that boyish stress of enchantment that this Ode and the *Lady of Shalott* and many other of his pieces once laid me under. Rose Hall, Lydiate (a country house where I sometimes spend a night as occasion requires and take the opportunity to write my letters). Jan. 11 1880. And here I must stop for tonight.

Jan.14 8 Salisbury Street, Liverpool—The new prosody, Sprung Rhythm, is really quite a simple matter and as strict as the other rhythm. Bridges treats it in theory and practice as something informal and variable without any limit but ear and taste, but this is not how I look at it. We must however distinguish its εἶναι and its εὖ εἶναι, the writing it somehow and the writing it as it should be written; for written anyhow it is a shambling business and a corruption, not an improvement. In strictness then and simple εἶναι it is a matter of accent only, like common rhythm, and not of quantity at all. Its principle is that all rhythm and all verse consists of feet and each foot must contain one stress or verse-accent: so far is common to it and Common Rhythm; to this it adds that the stress alone is essential to a foot and that therefore even one stressed syllable may make a foot and consequently two or more stresses may come running, which in common rhythm can, regularly speaking, never happen. But there may and mostly there does belong to a foot an unaccented portion or 'slack': now in common rhythm, in which less is made of stress, in which less stress is laid, the slack must be always one or else two syllables, never less than one and never more than two, and in most measures fixedly one or fixedly two, but in sprung rhythm, the stress being more *of* a stress, being more important, allows of greater variation in the slack and this latter may range from three syllables to none at all—*regularly*, so that paeons (three short syllables and one long or three slack and one stressy) are regular in sprung rhythm, but in common rhythm can occur only by licence; moreover may in the same measure have this

range. Regularly then the feet in sprung rhythm consist of
one, two, three, or four syllables and no more, and if for
simplicity's sake we call feet by Greek names, taking accent
for quantity, and also scan always as for rising rhythm (I call
rising rhythm that in which the slack comes first, as in iambs and
anapaests, *falling* that in which the stress comes first, as in
trochees and dactyls), scanning thus, the feet in sprung rhythm
will be monosyllables, iambs, anapaests, and fourth paeons,
and no others. But for particular rhythmic effects it is allowed,
and more freely than in common rhythm, to use any number of
slack syllables, limited only by ear. And though it is the virtue
of sprung rhythm that it allows of 'dochmiac' or 'antispastic'
effects or cadences, when the verse suddenly changes from a
rising to a falling movement, and this too is strongly felt by the
ear, yet no account of it is taken in scanning and no irregularity
caused, but the scansion always treated, conventionally and
for simplicity, as rising. Thus the line 'She had cóme from a
crúise, tráining séamen' has a plain reversed rhythm, but the
scanning is simply 'She had cóme | from a crúise | tráin | ing
séa | men'—that is/ rising throughout, having one monosyllabic
foot and an overlapping syllable which is counted to the first
foot of the next line. Bridges in the preface to his last issue says
something to the effect that all sorts of feet may follow one
another, an anapaest a dactyl for instance (which would make
four slack syllables running): so they may, if we look at the real
nature of the verse; but for simplicity it is much better to recog-
nize, in scanning this new rhythm, only one movement, either
the rising (which I choose as being commonest in English verse)
or the falling (which is perhaps better in itself), and always keep
to that.

In lyric verse I like sprung rhythm also to be *over-roveͅ*, that
is the scanning to run on from line to line to the end of the
stanza. But for dramatic verse, which is looser in form, I should
have the lines 'free-ended' and each scanned by itself.

Sprung rhythm does not properly require or allow of counterpoint. It does not require it, because its great variety amounts

to a counterpointing, and it scarcely allows of it, because you have scarcely got in it that conventionally fixed form which you can mentally supply at the time when you are actually reading another one—I mean as when in reading 'Bý the wáters of life where'er they sat' you mentally supply 'By thé watérs', which is the normal rhythm. Nevertheless in dramatic verse I should sparingly allow it at the beginning of a line and after a strong caesura, and I see that Bridges does this freely in *London Snow* for instance. However by means of the 'outrides' or looped half-feet you will find in some of my sonnets and elsewhere I secure a strong effect of double rhythm, of a second movement in the verse besides the primary and essential one, and this comes to the same thing or serves the same purpose as counterpointing by reversed accents as in Milton.

But for the εὖ εἶναι of the new rhythm great attention to quantity is necessary. And since English quantity is very different from Greek or Latin a sort of prosody ought to be drawn up for it, which would be indeed of wider service than for sprung rhythm only. We must distinguish strength (or gravity) and length. About length there is little difficulty: plainly *bidst* is longer than *bids* and *bids* than *bid*. But it is not recognized by everybody that *bid*, with a flat dental, is graver or stronger than *bit*, with a sharp. The strongest and, other things being alike, the longest syllables are those with the circumflex, like *fire*. Any syllable ending in *ng*, though *ng* is only a single sound, may be made as long as you like by prolonging the nasal. So too *n* may be prolonged after a long vowel or before a consonant, as in *soon* or *and*. In this way a great number of observations might be made: I have put these down at random as samples. You will find that Milton pays much attention to consonant-quality or gravity of sound in his line endings. Indeed every good ear does it naturally more or less/ in composing. The French too say that their feminine ending is graver than the masculine and that pathetic or majestic lines are made in preference to end with it. One may even by a consideration of what the music of the verse requires restore sometimes the pronunciation of Shakspere's time where it has changed and shew for instance that *cherry* must have been *cher-ry* (like *her*, *stir*, *spur*) or that *heavy* was *heave-y* in the lines 'Now the heavy ploughman snores All with weary task foredone'. You speak of the word *over*. The *o* is long no doubt, but long *o* is the shortest of the long vowels and may easily be used in a weak place; I do not however find that Tennyson uses it so in the Ode to Memory: in the line 'Over the dewy dark [or 'dark dewy'] earth forlorn'[1] it seems to be in a strong place.

I will inclose a little piece I composed last September in walking from Lydiate.[2] It is to have some plainsong music to it. I found myself quite unable to redeem my promise of copying you out the pieces you had not seen: time would not allow it. However I think you have seen them since in Bridges' book. Liverpool is of all places the most museless. It is indeed a most unhappy and miserable spot. There is moreover no time for writing anything serious—I should say for composing it, for if it were made it might be written.

I do not despair of our coming to meet, for business might perhaps bring you here. Meanwhile believe me your affectionate friend

GERARD M. HOPKINS S.J.

Jan. 14 1881.

You will then send the poems, I hope, as soon as possible. Jan. 16—I have added another piece, the *Brothers*.[3]

XII A

Hayton Vicarage, Carlisle. 24 Jan. 1881

MY VERY DEAR FRIEND,—I am infinitely delighted & relieved to receive from you a letter, & such a letter. Many thanks for your continued sympathy and interest. Your exposition of

---

[1]   Over the dark dewy earth forlorn.

[2] *Spring and Fall: to a young child* (Poems, 31). On account of variants this version is printed as NOTE E.

[3] This version, which shows many variants to *Poems*, 30, is printed as NOTE F.

Sprung Rhythm is profoundly valuable, & most lucid. I never rightly understood it before. I see now plainly what it is, as distinct from common & also 'counterpoint' rhythm: & it also seems to me that even if it s^d not be adopted generally (nor perhaps is that desirable or at all desired by you) it may do great good in poetry: in making writers careful. Some good present writers are not overstrong in the matter òf prosody. E.g. if I remember right, both M Arnold & Morris make *lyre* a dissyllable. I do not know whether that is one of the syllables that you w^d call 'circumflex' in accent. Tennyson is, I think, on the whole good in prosody: though I do not profess to be a great judge: but sometimes his pieces in irregular metres have a disappointing effect: e.g. The Sea Fairies. The verse that ends 'and the happy blossoming shore'[1] alwa̕ys seemed to me defective: but I may be wrong: probably am. By the way did you ever notice his counterpointed verse in one of the Idyls—

  'And the sword of the tourney acrofs her throat.'[2]

This is counterpointed, perhaps, in resemblance to

  'Burned after them to the bottomlefs pit.'[3]

and has besides one of those elisions (or else superfluous syllables) of which he is fond, but of which, as a rule, he only admits one in a verse. He is careful, or rather artificial, palpably so, in his prosody: & has not had on the whole the best influence. His fascinating power, of which & the cessation of which with advancing years, you give so perfect a rationale, used to be very wonderful. Maud was the last work in which it was exercised. The first Idyls, which came next I think, shewed a change of manner, which among his slaves was the signal of a servile war. I am glad you name the Lady of Shallot: for that is the best of the early poems—in fact the best of all: & still keeps its fascination for me. But look at the difference

---

[1] Whither away from the high green field and the happy blossoming shore? (Ed. of 1830, l. 8.) This line, that seems to foreshadow the *Lotos Eaters*, is unchanged, save for a comma, in the version of 1853.

[2] *Pelleas and Ettare*, p. 440 (*Works*, Macmillan, 1909).

[3] *Paradise Lost*, vi. 866.

of manner between that & Elaine: for instance in the floating
down of the boat to Camelot, where all is magical imagination
in the old piece, & all literal description & hard painting in
the new, not a detail left to the imagination.

I am glad to see that you so much younger a man went thro'
the Tennysonian fascination as well as those of older comprehension. The fact is, to end this, that Tennyson did invent a
new poetical diction: & he deserves full credit for it: but it was
a diction that was only applicable to a narrow range of subjects,
& he seems to have exhausted it & them. His diction fascinated
the world for long.

I wish you had more time for writing: it certainly does seem
a great pity, however valuable the other work that you do. I like
very much the two little pieces that you have sent: no one else
could have written them. It seems to me that in the couplet

> 'Nor mouth it, no nor mind exprefsed
> But heárt heárd of, ghóst guéssed:'

it would be an improvement to bring the latter line into common rhythm—

> But heart heard of it, ghost guessed.

Just there the poem seems to want to be very plain, as it gives
the leading, a very beautiful, thought. You will pardon me, I
know. Also, in the other truly charming piece, I c.ᵈ wish that
the first couplet finished the sense. It runs,

> How lovely is the elder brother's
> Love, all laced in the other's
> Being—

If it would go somehow,

> How lovely in the elder brother
> Love, all laced in the other.

Would not that be an improvement—I dont mean *that*, but
something like it, which you could do.

> How lovely in the elder brother
> The love, all laced in the other,
> Which he bears! I watched this well; &c.

This has just occurred to me, & I write it: you w.d get rid of
'I *have* watched this well', which seems not the right tense,
unlefs there be a full stop after well.

Thank you for your kind words of my own writings. They
gave me comfort when I needed it much. I need it still, & they
still give it. I send you some of my MS pieces & shall be only
too glad to have them criticised by you. Bridges has seen most
or all of them. One or two you will see to be additions to
Christ's Company. The piece called *Addrefs*[1] is to be before the
piece in my final vol. called *Loves Consolation*, if ever they are
reprinted: and that is to be followed by the tales in the two
volumes, & by those I now send; to form one series. Of these
last, of the one called Maurice[2] &c, the story is original: of the
other the story is altered from Elegant extracts, that old book,
where it occurs in prose & is attributed to 'a Byzantine author'.
I found out the other day that the Byzantine author was Oliver
Goldsmith—it is in his Essays. If I had known that, I should
have let it alone.[3]

I have some others which I may trouble you with some time.
The 'Epic',[4] which I rather call an Epic Sketch, came of my
being thrown many years ago among Germans, and others of
northern knowledge & tastes. It was written before I knew that
Morris was attending to northern myths, in fact most of it was
written before he began Jason, much more the Earthly Paradise.
This however does not affect him: for we are utterly different.
Have you seen his Sigurd—i.e. the poetical version in Alexandrines, or at least six-strefsed verses? Sigurd the Volsung.[5]

Bridges did not read much of the poem, & no wonder, for he
worried himself with the miscellaneous ones, far more than they
merited. I shall probably see him in London not long hence.

Believe me ever your affectionate friend

R. W. DIXON

[1] Unpublished, at all events under this title.
[2] If extant, in MS. In a later letter called *Love's Casuistry.*
[3] Printed posthumously (*Last Poems*) as *Too Much Friendship*. See p. 82, n. 3.
[4] Presumably a reference to one of the never-published 'northern epics'.
[5] Published in 1877 (1876).

[In pencil]

You will see Bridges pencil marks.

Make any observations or corrections that occur to you, on the blank sides.

I shall have to ask for their return.

XII B

Hayton Vicarage, Carlisle. 28 Mar. 1881

MY DEAR FRIEND—A Mr. Hall Caine, a stranger to me but friend of Rossetti's, has written for my consent to reprint a couple of my Sonnets in a large collection of Sonnets both already printed & not yet printed, which he is publishing.[1] It is a very important undertaking & he is evidently a man of very high poetical insight & ability, as it seems to me from something that he has sent, a paper on the Supernatural Imagination.[2]

In my reply I mentioned you—for he asked for any 'sonnet treasure' that I might know of: & have received from him a request to send him an example of your work. I send him today the two sonnets 'Starlight Night' & 'Skylark': not of course for publication without your consent: but for inspection; to gratify him. I now write to ask if you will consent that some sonnet of yours s^d be published with your name by him. If so,

---

[1] In a letter to Hall Caine (*Recollections*, 1882, p. 258) Rossetti writes (on the subject of sonnets and the projected anthology): 'There is an admirable but totally unknown living poet named Dixon. I will send you two small vols. of his which he gave me long ago, but please take good care of them, and return them as soon as done with. I value them highly. I forgot till to-day that he had written any sonnets, but I see there are three in one vol. and one in another. I have marked my two favourites. If I live, I mean to write something about him in some quarter when I can. His finest passages are as fine as any living man can do. He was a canon of Carlisle Cathedral, and at present has a living somewhere. If you wanted to ask him for an original sonnet, you might mention my name, and address him at Carlisle, with *Please forward*. Of course he is a Rev.'

[2] 'The Supernatural Element in Poetry', *New Monthly Magazine*, August 1879.

will you send him one—I think it had better be one in ordinary rhythm: or at most a counterpointed one: but of that you will judge.

Addreſs

> T. H. Hall Caine Esq
> 59 S. Chester Street,
> Liverpool.

His work is in the prefs. The post is closing. In extreme haste
Ever your friend

R. W. DIXON

XIII

April 6 1881. 8 Salisbury Street, Liverpool.

MY DEAR FRIEND,—I sent Mr. Hall Caine a choice of three sonnets, which he acknowledged and is to write 'at some length' shortly.

I take the opportunity to say something about the batch of poems you sent me. Time has been very short, especially since Lent came in, but I hope before very long to have studied them well.

The present remarks will be disjointed.

I find in the little lyrics a delightful freshness of out-of-doors, for instance in 'He wept, he wept'.[1] This poem brings not only before one's eyes the scene but it seems to raise as vivid 'phantasmata' in the other senses, as of cold and moisture.

On the other hand I could wish the key to the meaning in this and others were easier to find. It is slightly, but very slightly, indicated in their titles. For want of this they become, as a class of composition, riddles. Perhaps you wish this. Schiller has written some riddles of the sort, I believe; one about the Rainbow and so on.[2]

I do not think it would be possible to find, for a work of pure

---

[1] The beginning of *Death and Victory* (*S.P.*, pp. 152–3).

[2] *The Rainbow* opens Schiller's *Parabeln und Rätsel*, which, however, more resemble the Old English Riddles than R. W. D.'s poems.

imagination, anything anywhere more beautiful than *Fallen Rain*.[1] You must have been shocked at my objection from perspective. But thoughts of that sort haunt me. I have been setting airs to this piece and to 'Sky that rollest ever',[2] but unhappily I cannot at present harmonise them.

The poem 'Rise in their place the woods'[3] is beautiful in the same mournful vein as the Ode to Summer and there are others in the same. It contains one of the inimitable pathetic turns which attract me so much: 'They not regard thee, neither do they send' etc.

However the longest criticism I have to make at present is upon *Love's Casuistry*.[4]

You say that the plot of this piece is your own. It seems to me in general a hazardous thing, a pity, to make one's own plots: one cannot well have the independence, the spontaneousness of production which one gets from a true story or from a fiction that comes to one as a fresh whole not of one's own feigning. This piece it is plain has a *motive* and is planned to exhibit a certain situation, the situation which is darkly described in the opening. The consequence has been, as it seems to me, that you have invented *only just enough plot* to bring out the required situation. And this takes away from the interest. Besides motive a plot should have these two things, scenes and intrigue. By scenes I mean localisation, with local colour and particular details and keepings. These are things in which you naturally excel, as in the other tales of the set. But here there are scarcely any. If you had been treating some one else's plot you would have said something of what Basilis' house was like and where, but now you do not even tell us how she managed to get out of Venice into the wood without, as it would seem, crossing the water. There is also no intrigue. One wants to know how

---

[1] *S.P.*, pp. 148–9.

[2] *Wayward Water*: first published in *Lyrical Poems*, 1887, as *Song* (*S.P.*, p. 143).

[3] The opening of *The Fall of the Leaf*: first published in *Odes and Eclogues*, 1884 (*S.P.*, pp. 81–2).

[4] Presumably a poem that remained in MS.

Madaline happened to come up just when the two men had been fighting, and the hermit too, how he was there. The hermit is almost as bad as 'in the Queen's name I command you all to drop your swords and daggers'. I am afraid I shall have vexed you; nevertheless I believe you will see that I have hit a defect.

Easter Eve, which the Irish miscall Easter Saturday—In 'Margaret, are you grieving' will the following alteration do?—

> Nor mouth had, no, nor mind, expressed
> What héart héard of, ghóst gúessed.

The *Brothers* I have rewritten in deference to both yours and Bridges' criticisms and now he is not satisfied and wishes it back again. But I do not think I shall be able to send a corrected copy now. According to your wish I make it begin

> How lovely the elder brother's
> Life all laced in the other's!
> Love-laced; as once I well
> Witnessed, so fortune fell—

or something like that.

Mr. Hall Caine has not again been heard of.

Wishing you Paschal joy and a speedy conversion I remain affectionately yours

GERARD M. HOPKINS S.J.

Mr. Nicholas Pocock lately reviewed your second volume in the *Academy*,[1] but found much fault, except with the account of the dissolution of the monasteries.

April 19—I had meant to say something about *Cephalus and Procris*,[2] in which scenery, drawn with a masterly touch, is not wanting, but it is better no longer to delay sending this off.

---

[1] A very critical review—in $2\frac{1}{2}$ columns—of vol. ii (Henry VIII, 1538–47; Edward VI, 1547–8) in the issue of 12 Mar. 1881. For extracts from it see NOTE G. Pocock was the editor of Burnet.

[2] First published in *Odes and Eclogues* (*S.P.*, 83–91).

XIII A

Hayton Vicarage, Carlisle. 29 May 1881

My dear Friend.—I am home, & have been about ten days after a long and charming visit to Bridges, and taking Oxford on my way back. Bridges made an effort to get you up, & I should dearly have liked to see you, though so much changed myself that I do not suppose it possible that you could have seen any resemblance in me to what you may have in your mind, if indeed you retain the least recollection of me at Highgate.

It was whilst I was there, at Bridges', that your letter reached me, containing many kind things, some about those poems of mine which you have: & also some criticism which may be of ultimate value. It was at any rate very keen-sighted of you to see that there was a lack of àny reason how Maurice met Basilis for the second time in the Tale: for I had an account of it, & cut it out, because in narrative poems, as now done, there is so much of what I call *wooden* work,—accounts & explanations of how things came to paſs, how people got there & so on, when what is wanted is what they did when they were there. At present I still think this piece of joinery better out than in. I am touched & honoured by your thinking any of the short pieces worth setting to music. I hope one day to hear your airs. I have no musical ability myself, & regard those who have with great veneration. I am very glad that you like Cephalus & Procris.

You speak of the severe treatment of my 2nd Church History in the Academy. Mr. Pocock is a learnèd man, & an ardent lover of truth: but I think he did me an injustice, and that he is now conscious of it. I don't mean in what he said, but in what he left unsaid: for all his remarks referred to two chapters, not to the whole volume. I have had some correspondence with him, I may tell you in confidence: & I gather that he attacked me because he thought I was going to defend Edward VI's reformation. I am bound to defend nothing—my view is strictly

Richard Watson Dixon

historical: i.e. impartial: to expose basenefs & applaud goodnefs wherever I see it, though being an English Churchman,
I must write as one, i.e. having my point of view from the
interior of the English Church. With what Mr. Pocock actually
said, I do not agree, except in one instance in which he may be
right & I wrong, though even in that I might say something.
But the salient points of the volume, which, or some of which,
a reviewer should notice, are 1. The account of the dissolution
of the monasteries: never done before. 2. Henry's negotiations
with the Protestants; never done before. 3. The persecutions
under the Six Articles, never fully done before. 4 The liturgic
reformation, traced carefully step by step, which I think the
strong point of the English Reformation. To work out all these
has cost me great labour: & I cannot say that hitherto it has
been adequately received by the Press. There has been com-
mendation, but little real criticism. Mr. Pocock's was real
criticism, so far as it went. The professed Church of England
periodicals have been the most silent: the Guardian (weekly)
e.g. has hitherto cut both volumes altogether.

I felt very sorry that Mr. Hall Caine did not admit your
sonnets: but the loss is his. The more I study your work the
more I admire it: & the more I regret the fate by which, as
Bridges says, it still 'unfortunately remains in manuscript',[1] &
seems doomed to linger there.

I think that alteration of the beginning of the Brothers an
improvement: & hope that you do. It w^d not do to *begin* a
poem with a couplet running on—at least not *that* poem.

Every one about here is talking of Carlyle & his reminiscences.[2] I never understood why so much row has been made
over him & his works: why he was ever thought to have some
wonderful secret of life, which every one was to try to compre-
hend, the essence of it being that no one could. He was simply
a man of some genius, very painstaking. He never intended to
lead men: he only wanted to be read.

[1] See NOTE K, vol. i.
[2] Published in two vols. (edited by J. A. Froude) in 1881.

His writing always struck me as that of an ignorant man who had coached up one subject: and that not exactly a gentleman. He is often coupled with Ruskin, but there could not be a greater contrast. He spoiled Ruskin's style for him. I say all this: & yet I once wrote an article comparing & coupling the two:[1] but I was only 23 then. But I must not begin writing Reminiscences also. I have written a very egotistical letter as it is.

Yours always

R. W. DIXON

XIV

St. Joseph's, North Woodside Road, Glasgow. Sept. 16 1881.

MY DEAR FRIEND,—This, I hope, is the letter I have so long been meaning to write to you. I began one last night, but it did not do and this morning, as it happens, I had a letter from Bridges, who said you were desirous to hear from me.

I came here on the 10th of last month, to supply for a fortnight or so, but my stay has been prolonged and now I think will last almost till the time, Oct. 10th, when I am due at our noviceship, Manresa House, Roehampton, S.W., to begin my 'tertianship' or the third year of noviceship we make before taking our last vows. It is by rights however two months short of a year, this third year, and should end on Sept. 8 1882.

Now, my dear friend, I think, as I am north, north of you, we might somehow manage a meeting as I go south, if it were only an hour or so at Carlisle. It is to Liverpool I shall be going, to pack up, for I left almost all my things behind me; the journey is not so very long; and I could be in late, any time before half past ten at night would, absolutely speaking, do.

[1] Probably 'Gothic Art and John Ruskin', *London Quarterly Review*, January 1857; this review was edited by Thomas McNicoll, a friend of R. W. D. (see *Life of James Dixon, D.D.*, 1874, pp. 344–5). The article says of Ruskin and Carlyle: 'These two great men are not unnaturally to be regarded as the complement of one another'; and they are so regarded through three pages.

You could no doubt come in from Hayton on most days if
warned beforehand. Let me hear about this.

Bridges' convalesence is wearily slow. He is at Hampstead
now, where my family live, but they happen to be staying near
Winchester. I was in London in the summer and went to see
him: he could not talk long and I went away very gloomy and
sad at heart, and after that when I called I was not allowed to
go up.

I brought with me from Liverpool some but not all of your
poems; which I shall shortly be returning: indeed I ought to
have done so before, and you may be needing them. I have not
ventured to make any notes opposite them, as I think you wanted
me to do. We could speak of them if we met; still criticism is
more satisfactory on paper. I shall conclude, at least, with some
desultory remarks on them—but tomorrow or thereafter, for it
is bedtime.

Sept. 17—'Does the south wind'[1]—This is one of those inter-
pretations of the meanings of nature of which you have the
secret, like those princes and people in fairytales who 'knew
what the birds were saying.' Still *I* do not understand the
interpretation. The last stanza breathes a lovely touching
pathos—'more make to cease' lingers on the mind.[2] Now is this
it? In Nature is something that makes, builds up, and breeds,
as vegetation, life in fact; and over against this, also in Nature,
something that unmakes or pulls to pieces, what in another
place is called Death and Strife. This latter power must be
utterly unconscious, blind, and the other not; for if it were
otherwise this scene of havoc, strife, and defacement could not
go on. Now is that anything like? And I cannot be sure whether
'Earth's image of her toil' is the results of the toil, the manu-

---

[1] Printed posthumously, *S.P.*, p. 147; the title, *Ruffling Wind*, was given
by G. M. H.

[2] The last stanza is:

> O would they then come to spoil
> Sad Earth's image of her toil?
> O would they more make to cease
> Sweet Earth's mirror of her peace?

facture, as the leaf and the lily, or the picture of it, the shadow of woods and lawns in still water, the same as the 'mirror of her peace'.

'Sky that rollest ever'—I was quite inspired by this and have an air for it which I should like you to hear, for it is wholly fathered by the poem, but at present it is unharmonised. For the sake of a refrain I was forced to add this: 'Thou that hadst thy mirror In the yearning sea, Why wouldst thou love error More than constancy?' Will that, or something like it, do?[1] This poem will always be in my mind when I see blue and white in running streams ravelled and unravelled by the current. By the by, can the song be called 'Wayward Water'?[2]

'Fallen Rain'—I have spoken of this before. I had to repeat 'Why am I cast down' for a refrain.

'The Willow'[3] has the same command of pathos by direct and simple touches like 'mournful tears' and 'leaves of heavy care' which is to be remarked everywhere in your work and seems so easy and is so hard. We find it in the *Stabat Mater*, but Fr. Faber writing on the same theme could never command it.

'The Nile'[4]—The metre is, I think, your own invention and you have used it for eastern subjects before. It is imposing. It is strange to me that in a measure in which the rhythm requires to be so much marked you allow so much reversal of accent, as in the first line for instance and the third, or allow over-syllabling, as in 'oftentimes' where the verse wants 'ofttimes'.

---

[1] R. W. D.'s second stanza is:

> Truer is thy mirror
> In the lake or sea;
> But thou lovest error
> More than constancy.

[2] The last *Song* in *Lyrical Poems*, 1887: called *Wayward Water* in *S.P.*, pp. 143–4.

[3] Unidentified: not the well-known *Song*, beginning, 'The feathers of the willow'.

[4] This poem, if it exists, is in MS.

In measures like this there is always apt to come in something prosaic and *banal*, as Tennyson's ballads—*Lord of Burleigh* ('He was but a landscape painter'; where read 'undertaker', for it is the fact that Lord Burleigh passed himself of[f] as belonging to 'the black trade'), *Lady Clara Vere de Vere, Locksley Hall* etc., and I think you have not completely escaped it.

'The Old Bishop'[1] is a fine and insighted picture. 'Now knowing men' e.g. is a great stroke. The final couplet, if I understand it is a beautiful simile, but it is not explosive, as an epigram ought to be: do you not mean that fire leaves no corpse of itself behind it but is one moment burning fire and the next out and annihilated?

'The Mystery of the Body'[2] is something like the last and asks a very deep question. I find, if I may say so, here and in other places a certain want of rhetoric which makes a kind of meagreness or want of flush and fusedness in the diction.*

'What is beyond?'[3]—I do not feel sure I understand it. I take it literally, as a reflection on a hazy day and landscape: is there more? It has a delightful amplitude, breadth, of open air about it, as in 'home of lightning and of wind' and 'Light above it, air beneath'. The mountain like a curved moon I take to mean a mountain of rounded crest—rounded on one side and scooped or scarped away sharply on the other, as one often sees, so as to be like the horn of the crescent very near the end of·the first quarter. Is that right?

'The Spirit Wooed'[4] is a lovely piece of nature and imagination all in one, in a vein peculiarly yours: I do not believe there is anyone that has so much of Wordsworth's insight into nature as you have. Then it seems to me the *temper* is exactly right, a

* This 'flush' or fusion you supply by pathos or some such affection: where there is no affection concerned arises the kind of meagreness I complain of. I feel it in 'nerve' and 'curve'.

[1] This poem, if it exists, is in MS.
[2] Stands third in *Lyrical Poems* (*S.P.*, p. 109).
[3] If extant, in MS.
[4] *Ode: The Spirit Wooed*. The fifth of *Lyrical Poems* (*S.P.*, pp. 113–15).

thing most rare, which of Tennyson and Browning and most of our modern poets can by no means be said. The image of the moon's footfall is very beautiful. About the golden arms or arm of sunset I have a difficulty.[1] If the golden arms are arms of cloud gilded by the sun there is none; but if, as I rather fancy, it is arms as we speak of arms of the sea, golden channels or openings between the clouds, then I have that trouble of perspective which often haunts me. What it is I will not say now, for I want this to get off tonight, but will continue presently. In the meanwhile believe me your affectionate friend

GERARD M. HOPKINS S.J.

Sept. 17 1881. I find the post does not go tonight

Sept. 18—If the golden arms then are partings in the sunset clouds they are channels, hollows, or depressions, within which, not on which a head would have to be laid. I will give a glaring instance from Browning of false perspective in an image. In his *Instans Tyrannus* he makes the tyrant say that he found the just man his victim on a sudden shielded from him by the vault of the sky spreading itself like a great targe over him, 'with the sun's disk for visible boss'.[2] This is monstrous. The vault of heaven is a vault, hollow, concave towards us, convex upwards; it therefore could only defend man on earth against enemies above it, an angry Olympus for instance. And the tyrant himself is inside it, under it, just as much as his victim. The boss is seen from behind, like the small stud of a sleevelink. This comes

---

[1] The printed version has:

> Leanest thou thy head
> On sunset's golden breadth? . . .

[2] *Dramatic Romances, Instans Tyrannus*, vii. 1–8.

> When sudden . . . how think ye, the end?
> Did I say 'without friend'?
> Say rather, from marge to blue marge
> The whole sky grew his targe
> With the sun's self for visible boss,
> While an Arm ran across
> Which the earth heaved beneath like a breast
> Where the wretch was safe prest!

of frigid fancy with no imagination. If I am right in finding fault with your image it is a trifle, still it makes me uncomfortable.

The directness of *the Spirit Wooed* distinguishes it and other of your poems from Wordsworth's in the same kind: his are works of reflection, they are self-conscious, and less spontaneous, but then the philosophy in them explains itself the clearer on that account.

'Exeat'[1] is a beautiful and finished epigram in the sense of a riddle well *asked*. The answer I cannot guess. Sometimes I think the host is the body and the ruddy room the hue of health in the cheeks. However I can make nothing out of this.

I must now end and hope presently to write some more.

I think I must get my sister, who is an educated musician, to harmonise *Sky that rollest*[2] and so send it you. It is true it will not be exactly what I mean, but she will no doubt do it well and it will save time. I can afterwards please myself. The other piece is difficult and experimental, so I shall not send that.

XIV A

Hayton Vicarage, Carlisle. 22 Sept. 1881.

MY DEAR FRIEND,—I write a word to ask whether you could not manage to come here for a night or two on your way south. I shall be in Newcastle the week previous to the 10th October: but on that Monday shall be home. Indeed I return from Newcastle on the Friday before: so that if you came on Friday & stayed till Monday, the day on which your return is fixed, that would do: do better.

I am extremely obliged by your criticism: but it is too favourable. I shall look to hear the airs to which you have tuned the two you speak of. I can only wonder: for the faculty of composing a musical air is one that I am entirely destitute of.

What you say of meagrenefs is entirely true, & a thing in my diction of which I have been long conscious. It is however I

---

[1] Posthumously published: *S.P.*, p. 159.
[2] See Appendix III, 4a.

think fundamental in me: & can only receive occasional correction. It stands in contrast with what you happily call flush: the quality that you have in perfection & of which Bridges also is a great master. I am going to write to B. shortly. His illnefs is a distrefsing thing: but it must be expected to be slow. I had the same thing as a boy, & so know how slow recovery is.

Yours always affectionately

R. W. DIXON

XV

St. Joseph's, North Woodside Road, Glasgow. Sept. 24 1881.

I am writing with a 'stylographic' or fountain pen; it is a very convenient thing, but I am almost afraid the ink must be out.

MY DEAR FRIEND,—Thank you for your kind invitation: there is none I should so much like to avail myself of. But I am afraid it can hardly be. First of all I should explain that though I am to be at Roehampton on the 10th, that is by no means the day I shall be leaving Glasgow; indeed if I had to go all that way in one day I should never have thought of halting at Carlisle. I must go first back to Liverpool to pack and if possible to see some of my friends there; for which I should like a few days—days in the week before Oct. 10. My pen, I find, is empty.

Next I might not get leave. Still I might too and I could try.

But what weighs with me most is that if I were at Hayton I could not say mass, and hitherto since I have been ordained I have never missed doing so except when I could not help it. I am not willing to give up this principle now, but, after taking advice, I think I see what will be the best plan. I could leave Glasgow one day conveniently by the 10 o'clock train and be at Carlisle by half past twelve. I could leave it by the eight o' clock train (there is one thereabouts) and be at Preston, where we have three houses and the Rector is a good friend of mine and very hospitable, by eleven. That would leave me more than seven hours with you, if you were not away. Either we could

58

see Carlisle Cathedral or we could go down to Hayton. Perhaps you drive to and fro or there is a railway (I think not) or we could walk—it is seven miles, is it not? I shd. not like, if I could help it, to walk both ways, not being in good trim for that now, but I would if no other means presented itself; but such a walk of course is a great timewaster. This would be, I suppose, early next week. Write and say what you think. Surely it can be managed. I have a curiosity to see Hayton.[1] Moreover for the plan I propose either no leave is required or leave which would be certainly granted.

I will write no more criticism in this letter, but there was something in some letter of yours some while ago I wanted to return to, but now it has escaped me. It was, I think, about Carlyle. Your words surprised me '—of some genius': they would commonly be thought, and so they appear to me, too weak. I do not like his pampered and affected style, I hate his principles, I burn most that he worships and worship most that he burns, I cannot respect (no one now can) his character, but the force of his genius seems to me gigantic. He seems to me to have more humour than any writer of ours except Shakspere. I should have called him the greatest genius of Scotland. And yet after all I could fancy your making a good case against him, especially bearing the rule in mind *nemo coronabitur nisi qui legitime certaverit*: always to be affected, always to be fooling, never to be in earnest (for as somebody said, he is terribly earnest but never serious—that is never *in* earnest) is not to fight fair in the field of fame.

About your history we will speak. Believe me your affectionate friend

GERARD HOPKINS S.J.

---

[1] Hayton is a village built of reddish sandstone, with no pronounced character save Cumbrian stubbornness, winding irregularly up a slope. The church, dating from 1780, stands a little off the road on a slight rise, and is definitely not attractive (See R. B.'s *Memoir*, pp. xx–xxi.) Near it the vicarage, though pleasantly situated, with woods and hills in the background, looks shut in. The surrounding fields have tall hawthorn hedges. R. W. D. is still affectionately remembered in Hayton by older villagers.

XV A

Hayton Vicarage, Carlisle. 24 Sept. 1881.

MY DEAR FRIEND,—Can you come on Friday next? I fear that is the only day this week: for on the principle I suppose that if a good man ever does a bad thing he is instantly run down, squelched and variously finished, while a bad man does the like with habitual impunity, I, often more at leisure am just now under a prefs of engagements which renders it difficult to put before you that full choice of time which I might eleven months out of the twelve.

Or, could you come on Saturday, 8 October? That seems the only other alternative.

If you can do either of these days, & arrive in Carlisle about 12, I will also arrive in Carlisle about 12-30: we could see the Cathedral; go to Hayton by the 2 o'clock, and you could return to Carlisle thence by the 6-30, & so go on to Preston.

(My engagements this week are the Diocesan Conference tomorrow & Wednesday; a sermon for a Choir Festival at Wigton on Thursday, & a Sunday School treat at a place called Talkin on Saturday: thus leaving Friday for you. Next week, Monday go to Newcastle for Congress, return on Friday thus leaving Saturday for you.)

My place is half a mile from How Mill station on the N.E.R.

Carlyle was a humourist, but of a very limited range: as a writer his greatnefs lay in observation, & the collection of particulars: he could draw nothing universal: no rule, no teaching in him; & yet he put on the attire of a teacher. He was the greatest imposter, I think, that ever figured in literature:[1] so great that it required his own hand to expose him. I once admired him intensely: but not for long, I think: & I always felt a sort of secret surprise when Jones (especially & also Morris)

---

[1] Cf. M. Arnold (*Letters of Arnold to Clough*, ed. H. F. Lowry, 1932, letter of 23 Sept. 1849, p. 111): 'moral desperadoes like Carlyle'.

took him up with the wildest enthusiasm. I wish you would read something of his again, & then say what you think of it & him.

Ever your affec^{te} friend
R. W. Dixon

XVI

Sept. 26 1881. St. Joseph's, North Woodside Road, Glasgow.

My dear friend,—I shall continue jotting my remarks on your poems.

'Life and Death'[1]—The irregular opening verses may be scanned two ways and I do not know which is right: this is unsatisfactory. Death's lighting and then hiding the flame I take to mean the secret preservation of individual being in death (treated also in 'Dust and Wind').[2] These very subtle and original speculations, I may remark, as they follow out natural suggestions only and take no account of the supernatural have a quite heathen air; they remind one something of Empedocles and the early Ionian and Eleatic philosophy. I can make nothing of the final couplet 'My poppies are as red As the roses round his head'.[3] One would say the flowers should be allotted the other way; in Rossetti's picture the Sibylla Palmifera they are so: the death's-head is crowned with poppies and roses symbolise life. Perhaps if I understood the couplet this difficulty would be cleared up too. At present it is a skeleton epigram and sounds, as such, inconclusive: poppies *are* as red as, if anything redder than roses. The instances of life's work might perhaps be more striking and decisive; I fancy Empedocles or Heraclitus would have given more striking ones. Nevertheless this poem has charmed me among the most. 'Vermilion, saffron, white' is a brilliant stroke (that is a lie, so to speak, of Lessing's that pictures ought not to be painted in verse, a damned lie—so to speak). But why do *those* colours weave the delight?—as samples, I suppose, and as the gayest. And

---

[1] The fourth of *Lyrical Poems* (*S.P.*, pp. 110–12).
[2] *Last Poems*, pp. 23–7.   [3] This couplet was not printed.

more by token, Miss Rossetti in her new volume (I have not seen it, but I read this poem in the *Athenaeum*) has a piece called 'Symbols of Life and Death', I think, in which is quite a parallel line, 'Scarlet and golden and blue':[1] you should see this lovely poem. Some of the lines in Death's 'Legend' or address are deeply pathetic: 'In sorrow and in tears I ruin what she rears'. And the last couplet is fine in the extreme: yet the ear repines at the imperfect rhyme.[2]

'Dust and Wind'[3]—The irregular rhythm halts greatly, as Bridges, I see, has marked: one would say that the verse broke down under the burden of the thought. But this should not be: Tennyson's *Two Voices* is a philosophical poem written with the greatest flow, lucidity, and point. The thought is very interesting, but I do not feel comfortable about it: what is this resurrection to joy with pain? some doctrine of transmigration, the Buddhist 'Eightyfourthousand' and the Welsh Abred, is hinted at in this and several other poems. Or is the resurrection here spoken of not individual but merely the rising of another 'child of humanity' (as Fr. Clare my rector, who is a famous preacher, says many times in every one of his sermons) in the place of those who have gone before? There is one beautiful image, of 'the chilly roses of eve', and another of the archer, but one wants more: the *Two Voices* is bright with imagery. And the end is so inconclusive: *is* that the end on page 6 or is a sheet lost? The motive, namely the likeness of dust in the wind to the body inspired by the soul, is pregnant, but the poem does not give unmixed pleasure.

'Tameness'[4] is vivid as a picture and pathetic in feeling. But when did this deliverance take place? for it reads to me like what infidels say, but it cannot be so meant.

'Epigram'[4] on the stage. It seems to me that it might be and ought to be more pointed and explosive.

---

[1] *A Pageant and other Poems* (1881), *Mirrors of Life and Death*, p. 28: the line is: Scarlet or golden or blue.

[2]   But when I came to break
     The subtle bond, they shriek.

[3] *Last Poems*, pp. 23–7.   [4] If extant, in MS.

'The Rich Man to the Poor'[1] is flowing and beautiful. It is something like Patmore with his insight and delight in paradox on, so to say, the Tory side of everything. But it does not rest the mind: it is like Ecclesiastes without the epilogue.

'The Hand of Man'[2] has a kind of moistness of sorrow deeply charged through it. It might, I think, have more finish and sweeter and more satisfying cadences. Would it not be sweeter in eights and sixes? I seem to hear it more in Wordsworth's vein.

'The Unknown King'[3] I cannot make out, but it has something to do with 'Dust and Wind'. And certainly what I can make out I do not like. Neither are the verse and imagery rich enough, as it seems to me. 'Know as we are known' I have always understood | known of God, not of other men.

'The Woodpecker'[1] reminds one of Cowper's poems in this metre and has the same sort of 'instress' of feeling but not quite the same satisfactory cadences. 'As the leaf that is dead and was sere' is quite inconclusive.

'Asking'[1]—I can make nothing of this, there seems no clue at all. One foot lines are very difficult to manage: I do not think these are altogether successful ones. I see some kind of wooing of the Spirit of Nature, but to reveal what? And whose prayer is it?

'The Earth's Sun'[1] has the pathos and human sympathy which so many of these poems express, but the jaunt of the rhythm scarcely suits it. And there is surely a great want of imagery.

Much the same applies to 'Vain Ambition'.[4] 'White-armed fays' strikes me as quite unreal.

And to 'The World and Man',[5] which sounds very heathenish to me.

[1] If extant, in MS.
[2] Stands eleventh in *Lyrical Poems* (*S.P.*, pp. 124–5).
[3] *Last Poems*, pp. 33–4.
[4] Stands twelfth in *Lyrical Poems*.
[5] Is this perhaps *Nature and Man*, the sixth of *Lyrical Poems* (*S.P.*, pp. 116–20)?

'Unrest'[1] is very beautiful, but breathes downright despair. But surely morning cannot be rising over all lands. Why are the hands clasped? is it in grief or in prayer or the clench of resolution? there shd., I think, be some further determination of this.

'Man' ('The world was gay')[2] is very fine and grim, especially the last stanza. The dragons seem suggested by a passage in, I think, *In Memoriam*.

'The Silent Heavens'[3]—The thought is striking, but the rhythm to my ear unpleasing, mechanically mournful, and the diction not spontaneous.

The 'Secret Execution'[4] is truly brilliant. Still I could wish the rhythm and diction more finished and flowing. The stanza e.g. 'And turning back thy head' halts much.

'O ubi? Nusquam'[5] is deeply tender and full of the freshness and open air of evening landscape.

There are the same beauties in 'Winter will follow'.[6]

'To Fancy'[7] is striking and moving. I shd. have liked more precision of imagery.

'To Autumn'[8] seems perfunctory or slight.

Several Songs—These songs (which are more of pictures than songs and not all of them very well suited to be sung, as the delay of singing is apt to scatter the images and break up the perspective and completeness of the picture) are to me like photographs of the imagination, like photographs or as much of a landscape as one sees by chance through the square of a window in passing, vivid pieces of nature but without centrality or reference to one point. 'Thou sleepest now, O wind'[8] reminds one, which is a rash challenge, of 'Blow, blow, thou winter wind'—in sound, for the thought is as different as it is

[1] The thirteenth of *Lyrical Poems* (*S.P.*, pp. 126–7).
[2] *Man's Coming*: stands fourteenth in *Lyrical Poems* (*S.P.*, pp. 128–9).
[3] Printed posthumously: *Last Poems*, pp. 30–1.
[4] Extant in MS.   [5] Printed posthumously: *S.P.*, pp. 150–1.
[6] Stands fifteenth in *Lyrical Poems* (*S.P.*, pp. 130–1).
[7] Stands seventeenth in *Lyrical Poems* (*S.P.*, pp. 136–7).
[8] If extant, in MS.

beautiful. 'Through the clearness of heaven'[1] has a lovely freshness, but the anapaests are somewhat loaded and the rhythm straggling. 'Oh, bid my tongue'[2] is something like Byron's lyrics, but certainly wants something: as it stands it seems to me imperfect, falling short of epigram. I believe it would be bettered by 'tautening' the measure—'Bid my tongue be still, Bid mine eyes be dry' perhaps.

'False Mark'[3] is vivid and eerie, but not as a whole so interesting as 'Lord Ronald and fair Ellen both'.[4]

'Both less and more'[5] I cannot understand. It suggests the 'Vision of Sin'. Though it is often done, I can never be reconciled to calling men or women angels; there seems something out of tune in it.

I hope my telegram was in time this morning. I sent it at about halfpast eight or a quarter to nine. I found that Brampton was the nearest telegraph station, but how near Hayton I had no means of learning, so I assumed it to be 2 miles and paid accordingly. It was only yesterday evening that my plans were disarranged. I am afraid now we shall not meet. It is a sad pity.

I will send more criticisms presently. I am afraid they are too free. Believe me your affectionate friend

GERARD M. HOPKINS S.J.

My sister will no doubt harmonise my air and then you shall have it. At Inversnaid (where Wordsworth saw the Highland Girl) on Wednesday I was delivered of an air to 'Does the South Wind'[6] and jotted it down on Loch Lomond.

Sept. 30 1881.

XVII

Oct. 3 1881. St. Joseph's, North Woodside Road, Glasgow.

MY DEAR FRIEND,—Of the *Christ's Company* poems I admire in *St. John the Baptist*[3] the justice of the thought, but find the diction somewhat tame, often less than elegiac and much like

[1] The twenty-first of *Lyrical Poems* (*S.P.*, p. 141).
[2] Published posthumously: *S.P.*, p. 158.   [3] If extant, in MS.
[4] *C.C.*, *Ballad*, pp. 110–12.   [5] The tenth of *Lyrical Poems* (*S.P.*, p. 123).
[6] *Ruffling Wind* (*S.P.*, p. 147).

a stately prose: St. John might have said these things, but he would have said them with more enthusiasm, as we see by comparing the passage about the vipers with his words in the Gospel. I never heard about those Sons of the Unhappy: where does one read of them? 'Unsublime despair' though it may say just what was to be said is so modern that it grates. But I admire most the following stanzas about the Essenes: the diction now gathers nerve and flow. Perhaps the easiness and indeed nondescriptness of the metre injures the style. I must not object to *underneath*, *bequeath*, *death*, three bad rhymes, because I find that some people sincerely like them. I believe you are wrong about the local colouring: the wilderness of the Holy Land itself is waste, untilled land, 'bush', not sand.

St. Paul in Arabia[1]—Neither is this metre very interesting, though I like it better than the last. The thought *is* interesting, but it seems to me random and unconnected; perhaps I miss the clue. It is not characteristic of St. Paul; still he may in his many thoughts have had some like these. 'I cannot count the atoms placed Beneath my foot' is to me prosaic. The thought is here your favourite dust- or sand-thought. The second stanza about the making of mould from rock is the most beautiful and poetical, I think, in the piece.

The Other Mary[1] turns gracefully on this 'otherness' and the last stanza is especially felicitous, though for myself I believe it was all one woman, Mary Magdalen. You seem to me however to be in some way straitened by your quaintness in this poem. *Lord* and *broad*: shocking vulgarism!

The Last Supper[1] and *James and Jude*[1] have the same freakish and almost perverse beauty as the mystery in Longfellow's *Golden Legend* and some of your own earlier *Christ's Company* pieces. Still I find less pleasure than I once used in this kind: I half think that archaic quaintness is a fallacy, that nothing was ever quaint in its time. Besides in reproducing it one is liable to fall into solecisms. I have found that Chaucer's scanning, once understood, is extremely smooth and regular, much more

[1] If extant, in MS.

so than is thought by Mr. Skeat and other modern Chaucerists, and they think it regularity itself compared to what Dryden and older critics thought of it. So perhaps of the sort of thing you are here reproducing. All classic names were treated as coming to us thro' French and therefore as bearing the accent indifferently on any syllable; 'Andréw, Philíp, Barthóleméw'[1] will thus be correct and almost monotonously smooth and 'Thaddéus, Símon, ánd Judás', but 'Matthew and Thomas and James abide' will have a syllable too much, which in this simple undeveloped style is probably unlawful: it might be 'Matthéw [or Mátthew], Thomás, and Jámes abíde'. But now when one finds that it is all a matter of obsolete accent the quaintness, the rude but pleasing counterpoint, the irregularity, and the interest have all disappeared.

Iscariot[2] is very grim and powerful and the effect most legitimate. I take this and the two before to be sort of 'legends', such as might be written on scrolls issuing from the mouths of the characters. It is a peculiar and little worked branch of letters and has something Greek about it.

The *Address*[2]—In all this feeling and beautiful piece there is a certain shortcoming in the execution, which makes it imperfect. For instance its character depends a good deal on the roundel–like repetition and the success of this again depends on the happy variation of the context and sense in the refrain itself or else on its emphatic iteration in the same context and sense.* But these effects are not everywhere secured with a certain hand; for instance it is hard to say whether the sense varies or does not vary in 'Intent to prove': now that is unsatisfactory, as it would be if one said/ I cannot tell you whether those notes are in unison or not—they would not indeed be far apart but neither is their sameness marked: now they shd. be either in unison or at a known interval. 'For whoso fails' is a graceful play, 'A long farewell' is a successful reiteration, but 'Beyond compare'

* In which the French poets, I believe, excel.

[1] Spelt thus in MS.　　　　　[2] If extant, in MS.

has an uncertainty. 'And part are got . . . own heart' is noble, much from its plainness, but the mixed metaphor of 'wind' and 'mast' which follows is unsatisfying.

Terror[1] is a somewhat slight sample of that instress which is felt in the *Wizard's Funeral*[2] and many other places. I take it as a prayer to be 'spirited gently'.[3]

Death and Victory (I have spoken of this) and *The Storm Demon*[4] are in your finest style. I take them as dramatisings of the phenomena of weather, but I cannot follow quite all the turns and do not understand that angel or those angels that 'had joy'. Between these pieces flushed with colour and emotion and the *St. John Baptist* there is much difference.

Cephalus and Procris[5] is drawn with a broad and masterly touch, as in 'Seeking his way . . . grey-winged mist', and is a very fine piece. The freak of *Erechtheus* and *Orithyia* accented so I do like, but with a vicious taste, as for Stilton or high game: the remarks above apply. The satyr-scene is exquisite and all your own. Artemis' speech, good as it is, still seems to me to fall short of what narrative, that difficult art, may reach. It is inconsistent to say Artemis and then Aurora, but perhaps you had reasons for using the more familiar personification of Dawn.

Conflicting Claims[6] is to me a poem of an immortal beauty, *being* the very things that in others it praises. In 'Beauty, the heart of beauty'—down to 'have rest' and in the 'joys as keen as fears' and the 'rapturous frown' what lovely touches! But the first stanza is the least excellent and might, I fancy, be lighted up.

For tonight this must do. I am to go to Liverpool on Wednesday and to Roehampton on Saturday the 8th.

Your affectionate friend

GERARD M. HOPKINS S.J.

---

[1] Published posthumously, *S.P.*, p. 160.

[2] *C.C.*, p. 60 (*S.P.*, pp. 14–15).　　　[3] *The Tempest*, Act I, Sc. 2, l. 298.

[4] The seventh of *Lyrical Poems*.

[5] The fourth of *Odes and Eclogues* (*S.P.*, pp. 83–91). G. M. H. inadvertently wrote 'Proclis'.

[6] The first ode in *Odes and Eclogues* (*S.P.*, pp. 77–80).

XVIII

Manresa House, Roehampton, London, S.W.
[*c.* 11 October 1881][1]

MY DEAR FRIEND,—I am now at my old noviceship and am a novice again. This second probation lasts ten months, ending on St. Ignatius' feast July 31. We see no newspapers nor read any but spiritual books. In Lent we go out to give retreats and so on; beyond that *in eremo sumus*.

I had hoped to have finished my remarks on your poems and returned them before coming here, but could not quite. A few smaller pieces and the two longer ones remain, which in a few days I will forward with all the rest. The criticisms will be such as I can snatch time for. They ought indeed all to have been made long before. But I was jaded and kept putting things off. In this retirement the mind becomes both fresh and keen. I have no time now to write more.

What a sad pity I could not see you at Carlisle! Believe [me] yours affectionately

GERARD HOPKINS S.J.

XVIII A

Hayton Vicarage, Carlisle, 11 Oct. 1881.

MY DEAR FRIEND,—I cannot say how much I value your criticism on my poems: which is in fact inestimable, both in itself & in giving me a notion of their comparative value among themselves. I mean that I do not think them all worth publishing, & it is well to know which of them strike you as the most faulty. On the whole your judgment goes with mine, so far as you have yet exprefsed it. I always had doubts about the Unknown King,[2] & have somehow lost the clue of it. The same of Dust & Wind,[3] though that is a better piece, I think: but the metrical defects are great, & the spirit not the best. The same of S. Paul in

---

[1] Undated: this is R. B.'s pencilled suggestion.
[2] *Last Poems*, pp. 33–4.
[3] Ibid., pp. 23–7.

Arabia:[1] I have lost the clue of that: but it is very disjointed as it is. Your praise of some other pieces is, I fear, too great. I will not say too kind, because I know that it is simply sincere. But you think more of them than they deserve. I hope however that, at your own time, you will continue to note the others: for your remarks are invaluable.

I am very sorry to have mifsed you: it was a horrid concatenation that led to that. So you are entering on your last year of novitiate. I suppose you are determined to go on with it: but it must be a severe trial—I will say no more.

I had a note from Bridges, who is at Torquay, last week. He is getting on, but very slowly: his weaknefs great.

With what you say of 'false perspective' in Browning, I am inclined to agree—certainly in the instance you give: & I fancy it is a thing not unusual in him. But I s^d hardly accuse him of frigid imagination; or rather, as you have it, 'frigid fancy with no imagination': but perhaps you do not mean this as a general judgment on him. I have been reading his last volume, which he calls by the monstrous name of Dramatic Idyls.[2] They are all very bad (First Series is what I have). I cannot scan many of the verses in Phidippides any way, nor in some others. Do you know them? The Ring & Book[3] seemed to me to shew a failure in Browning's power, which is confirmed by his subsequent productions: & manifests itself in these ways. 1. Loss of form, with every kind of monstrosity. 2. The impotent remarking of particulars: as when he observes that the names of Wiseman, Newman, and Manning all contain the word man. 3. Preaching instead of teaching. Whole pages of the Bk and Ring preach, and there is nothing to be learned out of it. Even in Browning's best works I always had an indefinable feeling that he was not thoroughly educated; i.e. that he had not taken poetry at the highest point at which it had been left by others, and so was, as it were, off the track.

[1] If extant, in MS.
[2] The First Series was published in 1879, the Second Series in 1880.
[3] Published, in four vols., in 1868.

This is a very stupid letter. I wish I could exprefs how much I think of you, & feel with you, & how grateful I am for your criticism & opinion. Let me hear again at your leisure; or, if it occur to me, I will write again.

I am, my dear Friend,

Ever Yours affect^ly

R. W. DIXON.

XIX

Manresa House, Roehampton, London, S.W.

(By the by have you read Lothair?[1] because this house is the divine Theodora's: some of the scenes are laid here.) Oct. 12 1881.

MY DEAR FRIEND,—Some of the sonnets are very, I must say unpardonably, licentious in form. I recognise stricter and looser forms and the Shakespearian sonnet, though it is a sonnet only *in genere* and not one if by sonnet you mean the Italian sonnet, which is the sonnet proper—but this is a question of names only—the Shakespearian sonnet is a very beautiful and effective species of composition in the kind. But then, though simpler, it is as strict, regular, and specific as the sonnet proper. Moreover it has the division into the two parts 8+6, at all events 4+4+4+2. Now it seems to me that this division is the real characteristic of the sonnet and that what is not so marked off and moreover has not the octet again divided into quatrains is not to be called a sonnet at all. For in the cipher 14 is no mystery and if one does not know nor avail oneself of the opportunities which it affords it is a pedantic encumbrance and not an advantage. The equation of the best sonnet is

$$(4+4)+(3+3) = 2.4+2.3 = 2(4+3) = 2.7 = 14.$$

This means several things—(A) that the sonnet is one of the works of art of which the equation or construction is unsymmetrical in the shape $x+y = a$, where x and y are unequal in

[1] One of Disraeli's last novels, published in 1870.

71

some simple ratio, as 2:1, 3:2, 4:3: perhaps it would be better to say $mx+nx = a$. Samples of this are the Hexameter and Ionic Trimeter, divided by their caesura, as St. Austin *De Musica* suggests, so as to give the equation $3^2+4^2 = 5^2$ (it is not very clear how he makes it out, but at all events they give the equation $2\frac{1}{2}+3\frac{1}{2} = 6$ or $5+7 = 12$). The major and minor scales again consist of a pentachord + a tetrachord and in Plainsong music all the 'Authentic' Modes have this order and all the 'Plagal' the reverse, the tetrachord first. And I could shew, if there were time, that it would be impracticable to have a ratio of the sort required with numbers higher than 4 and 3. Neither would $4 : 2$ do, for it wd. return to $2 : 1$, which is too simple. (B) It is divided symmetrically too in multiples of two, as all effects taking place in time tend to be, and all very regular musical composition is: this raises the 7 to 14. (C) It pairs off even or symmetrical members with symmetrical (the quatrains) and uneven or unsymmetrical with uneven (the tercets). And even the rhymes, did time allow, I could shew are founded on a principle of nature and cannot be altered without loss of effect. But when one goes so far as to run the rhymes of the octet into the sestet a downright prolapsus or hernia takes place and the sonnet is crippled for life.

I have been longer and perhaps more dogmatic than I shd. have been over this point. Of the sonnets themselves those on the World,[1] except for happy touches, do not interest me very much and that to Corneille has a certain stiffness, as the majority of Wordsworth's have, great sonneteer as he was, but he wrote in 'Parnassian', that is the language and style of poetry mastered and at command but employed without any fresh inspiration: and this I feel of your sonnet here. The rest, that to George Sand and those on Shakespeare and Milton, are rich in thought, feeling, and diction.

On a Young Bird etc.[2]—This is a truly touching and finished

[1] A sonnet called *The World and its Workers* was printed posthumously, *S.P.*, pp. 163–4. The other sonnets mentioned are, if they exist, in MS.
[2] If extant, in MS.

little piece, the tale told with great flow and simplicity: the
pathos of a little tale like this is unique as a welltold jest and
has its own point as that has.   There are however two flaws
worth noticing.   It seems to me strange and, I think, unlawful
to call a 'naked floor' a 'bower': a bower is a *camera*, an arched
shelter whether of boughs or of cieling.   Also stanza 4. begins
with the same rhyme as 3. ends with, which is an awkwardness.

Ode on the Death of Dickens[1] is fine and stirring; the Aryan
image of the cloud cows and the dog particularly striking;[2] but
the anapaests are heavily loaded.   For myself I have been
accustomed to think, as many critics do, that Dickens had no
true command of pathos, that in his there is something mawkish; but perhaps I have not read the best passages.   Just such
a gale as this poem paints is blowing today (Oct. 14) and two
of my fellow Tertians have been injured by the fall of almost
half a tall cedar near my room, which wrecked the woodshed
where they happened to be and battered and bruised them with
a rain of tiles.

The Fall of the Leaf—I have spoken of this beautiful poem
before.

I cannot remember if I spoke of *Nature and Man*,[3] the one
beginning 'Blue in the mists all day'.   At all events it is one of the
most perfect of all, both in thought and expression.   The thing
had to be said.   I suppose 'pod' means some pod-like bud, for I
think, scientifically speaking, the pod is only a seed vessel.

There only remain the two tales; of which I will write another
day, though it must be less fully than they deserve.   I will
finish with remarks called out by your most welcome letter of
yesterday.

---

[1] *Last Poems*, p. 32.
[2]   the blasts urge
               From the depth of their grey mysterious cave,
               The white precipitate clouds, that seem made
               More slowly to wander the sky, like a herd
                   Of deep-uddered cows hotly bayed
               By a fierce dog beyond their own pace: . . .
[3] The sixth of *Lyrical Poems* (*S.P.*, pp. 116–20).

In speaking of 'frigid fancy' I referred to the particular passage only. But Browning has, I think, many frigidities. Any untruth to nature, to human nature, is frigid. Now he has got a great deal of what came in with Kingsley and the Broad Church school, a way of talking (and making his people talk) with the air and spirit of a man bouncing up from table with his mouth full of bread and cheese and saying that he meant to stand no blasted nonsense. There is a whole volume of Kingsley's essays which is all a kind of munch and a not standing of any blasted nonsense from cover to cover. Do you know what I mean? The *Flight of the Duchess*, with the repetition of 'My friend', is in this vein. Now this is *one* mood or vein of human nature, but they would have it all and look at all human nature through it. And Tennyson in his later works has been 'carried away with their dissimulation.'[1] The effect of this style is a frigid bluster. A true humanity of spirit, neither mawkish on the one hand nor blustering on the other, is the most precious of all qualities in style, and this I prize in your poems, as I do in Bridges'. After all it is the breadth of his human nature that we admire in Shakespeare.

I read some, not much, of the *Ring and the Book*, but as the tale was not edifying and one of our people, who had been reviewing it, said that further on it was coarser, I did not see, without a particular object, sufficient reason for going on with it. So far as I read I was greatly struck with the skill in which he displayed the facts from different points of view: this is masterly, and to do it through three volumes more shews a great body of genius. I remember a good case of 'the impotent collection of particulars' of which you speak in the description of the market place at Florence where he found the book of the trial: it is a pointless photograph of still life, such as I remember in Balzac, minute upholstery description; only that in Balzac, who besides is writing prose, all tells and is given with a reserve and simplicity of style which Browning has not got. Indeed I hold with the oldfashioned criticism that Browning is not really a

[1] Galatians ii. 13.

poet, that he has all the gifts but the one needful and the pearls
without the string; rather one should say raw nuggets and rough
diamonds. I suppose him to resemble Ben Jonson, only that
Ben Jonson has more real poetry.

As for Carlyle; I have a letter by me never sent, in answer to
a pupil of mine, who had written about him, and I find I there
say just what you do about his incapacity of general truths. And
I always thought him morally an impostor, worst of all impostors
a false prophet. And his style has imposture or pretence in it.
But I find it difficult to think there is imposture in his genius
itself. However I must write no more criticism.

I see you do not understand my position in the Society. This
Tertianship or Third Year of Probation or second Noviceship,
for it is variously called in the Institute, is not really a noviceship
at all in the sense of a time during which a candidate or proba-
tioner makes trial of our life and is free to withdraw. At the end
of the noviceship proper we take vows which are perpetually
binding and renew them every six months (not *for* every six
months but for life) till we are professed or take the final degree
we are to hold, of which in the Society there are several. It is
in preparation for these last vows that we make the tertianship;
which is called a *schola affectus* and is meant to enable us to
recover that fervour which may have cooled through application to study and contact with the world. Its exercises are
however nearly the same as those of the first noviceship. As
for myself, I have not only made my vows publicly some two
and twenty times but I make them to myself every day, so that
I should be black with perjury if I drew back now. And beyond
that I can say with St. Peter: To whom shall I go? *Tu verba
vitae aeternae habes.* Besides all which, my mind is here more at
peace than it has ever been and I would gladly live all my life,
if it were so to be, in as great or a greater seclusion from the
world and be busied only with God. But in the midst of outward occupations not only the mind is drawn away from God,[1]
which may be at the call of duty and be God's will, but

[1] For 'holy th', cancelled.

unhappily the will too is entangled, worldly interests freshen, and worldly ambitions revive.[1] The man who in the world is as dead to the world as if he were buried in the cloister is already a saint. But this is our ideal.

Our Rector Fr. Morris shd. be known to you as a historian in your own field and epoch of history.

Believe me your affectionate friend

GERARD M. HOPKINS S.J.

Oct. 17 1881.

XX

Manresa House, Roehampton, S.W. Oct. 23 '81.

MY DEAR FRIEND,—The first of December will be the three hundredth anniversary of the glorious martyrdom of Frs. Campion, Sherwin, and Bryant, Jesuits: would that something could be done in honour of the day. When at Glasgow I began an ode in their honour (not that I think much of writing odes as a means of honouring the saints), but got not far with it nor was much pleased with what I had done; it might have turned out well if time and other things had suited; but now it is laid aside.[2]

I will now turn to *Love's Casuistry*.[3] I still hold that there shd. have been more plot, more intrigue of plot, and at least more scenery. As it stands it is a chain of scenes, of interviews, without background, keepings, or scenery. Now it is a tale you are writing, not a play: in a play these things are supposed and supplied for you; in a tale you must yourself supply them. There are vivid touches, as about Basilis' vacant and beadlike eyes under her coif; one would like more of them.

There is also a touch of the sensational and incredible in Basilis' death: the chantry priest brings in his verdict of 'while in a state of unsound mind' with the simplicity of a juror. Could not some indication of her state be given before? See later.[4]

---

[1] For 'reawake', cancelled.
[2] See vol. i, p. 135. No part of this ode seems to have survived.
[3] If extant, in MS.
[4] These two words were added afterwards: see p. 79.

The whole poem is an admirable example of that sequence of feeling of which you are such a master. I shd. have to quote half of it to say this in detail. Some instances which especially strike me are 'But Oh, Basilis, Silence' etc; Love standing by and hating his liegeman; 'Now, Basilis, to thee I say no less'; the laboured and piteous repetition of 'And thou the same'; the turns of Basilis' first seizure on board ship and her passing pity for Cossimo (should it not be *Cosimo*?) when he ran after her; ' 'Twas love that slew her, miserable love'; 'Heaping huge strokes' etc. The imagery, though sparing, is most beautiful and in your happiest vein: nothing could better the richness, the imaginative reality, of the figures of the eagle and[1] the dove (Miss Rossetti has in the poem I lately quoted a noble passage beginning 'Like an eagle, half strength and half grace, Harrying the East and the West')[2] or of the moose and glutton. (I think the images I like best of all are in *Love's Consolation*, about the quicksilver[3] and the heart combed round with hair).[4] But 'lips the hue of lead' seems to me unreal; at least I never saw the lips change colour from emotion, but I may be wrong. And 'Each drop more precious than the gems that stud An angel's crown' strikes me as poor, indeed vulgar; I think angels are the very cheapest things in literature.

Odds and ends—At page 3 are four lines on one rhyme running: it seems an oversight. I cannot quite understand how

---

[1] MS. 'in'.

[2] *A Pageant and other Poems* (1881), *Mirrors of Life and Death*, p. 27. See p. 62, and NOTE H.

[3] *C.C.*, p. 88 (*S.P.*, p. 31):
> 'Tis better so, than never to have been
> An hour in love; than never to have seen
> Thine own heart's worthiness to shrink and shake,
> Like silver quick, all for thy lady's sake,
> Weighty, with truth, with gentleness as bright.

[4] *C.C.*, p. 98 (*S.P.*, pp. 47–8):
> and of us some
> About our hearts meshed the loved hair with comb
> Of our great love, to twine and glisten there,
> And when 'twas stiffened in our life blood dear,
> Then was it rent away; . . .

Maurice came to draw his hand across Basilis' eyes; it seems a strange uncalled-for thing to do, though it leads to a beautiful image. In the same scene you speak of the road and later of the floor: was it then in or out of doors that they met? It is as I complain, that there is no scenery, nothing localised. This is ambiguous: 'The tasselled sprays fence in the wind and fill Their souls with mimic fight'. One would take 'fence in' to mean *hedge in*, but the next line suggests that you mean *fence with one another in the wind*. 'Amity' is a poor word for *friendship*; it means more the absence of enmity.

The rhythm—You employ that lightsome French or Chau-cerian rhythm (though Chaucer properly read is heavier stressed than we think) with frequent inversion of accent (not really counterpoint) which Keats brought in (there are good instances of it in his *Cap and Bells*, a poem which in general drift however is so senseless, such a piece of nonsense that I had not patience to read it through: he has 'Besides, manners forbid that I should stay' or something like that, where the word *manners* reverses the accent even of the second foot, next to the fifth, the most sensitive and unalterable place in the 5-foot line; but the stress on the last syllable of *besides* carries it very grace-fully off). This rhythm suits the style and you wield it easily; still in certain connecting passages, where reflections occur, it is a little languid. The more we moralise the more does the style tend to be gnomic, sententious, epigrammatic and the verse crisp and terse. For this reason I find the opening of *Too Much Friendship*[1] (indeed much of it) unsatisfactory, as if it hung between two stools, two styles. In the present poem I think it unlawful or a mistake to mingle the two systems of rhythm, the fixed and counted French system with the modern freer soluble or equal-time system employed by Tennyson, according to which two syllables may be treated as equal to one long and so accentual dactyls or anapaests take the place of trochees and iambs and so on. But you do this in a line beginning with the anapaest 'From his hánd' and in others. Each system has its

[1] *Last Poems*, pp. 1–21.

beauties, but they ought not to be confused. And I agree with what Bridges has marked.

Oct. 25—I must withdraw or restate what I said about Basilis' death. We do see clearly enough that she is distraught beforehand (though I cannot follow the hermit's theology: it is plain she wrought herself into madness and that by a selfish and injurious indulgence of passion), and the objection I feel is to a certain inartistic patness about the hermit's explanation or even presence. It wd. be in place if the tale were as short as the argument prefixed to a play, but seems violent and unprepared on the scale of this poem. Still I do not wish any alteration, for the poem would not well bear lengthening and perhaps wd. lose by any changes. The tale is to illustrate a *motive*; it may, if you will not mind, be called the Four-lover Problem: Black Queen to play and mate in three moves. This is the problem in its simplest form, for one of the others might love cross too. They stand thus:

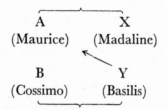

$$
\begin{array}{cc}
\text{A} & \text{X} \\
\text{(Maurice)} & \text{(Madaline)} \\
\text{B} & \text{Y} \\
\text{(Cossimo)} & \text{(Basilis)}
\end{array}
$$

The first move is / Basilis falls in love with Maurice and gives check. The next indispensable move is Cossimo's, who is left exposed. The third is mate. To these, which are strictly necessary, you add one move, one scene, more, which is where Maurice, so to say, tries to cover check. This shews how undisguisedly the story springs from, and is, its motive.

About *Too Much Friendship* I must be shorter.

Believe me now your affectionate friend

GERARD M. HOPKINS S.J.

Oct. 25 1881.

XX A

Hayton Vicarage, Carlisle. 26 Oct. 1881.

My dear Friend,—I shall not attempt to thank you for your invaluable criticism, but simply write about it, about the two Letters which I have had from you, on one or two points. But first, I hope that you are going on with poetry yourself. I can understand that your present position, seclusion and exercises would give to your writings a rare charm—they have done so in those that I have seen: something that I cannot describe, but know to myself by the inadequate word *terrible pathos*—something of what you call temper in poetry: a right temper which goes to the point of the terrible; the terrible crystal. Milton is the only one else who has anything like it: & he has it in a totally different way: he has it through indignation, through injured majesty, which is an inferior thing in fact. I cannot tell whether you know what I mean.

As to your criticisms: as to Sonnets. It has not been practised much by me: & you know that there are great temptations to abandon the regular form: but your determination of the matter is most forcible: you demonstrate the regular form to be the most beautiful: and I am not sure that if I try again I shall not keep to it. At all events the division into 8 & 6, as to rhyme, seems desirable, to avoid 'hernia'. Do you give much weight to Surrey and Spenser? they tried all sorts of things. In fact, if the regular sonnet be the prevailing Italian form which they knew, it w^d be curious to make out the various ways in which they (& others) varied from it, or tried to have in English something like it, or representing it: i.e. doing in English what it did in Italian, but yet not the same. They were the men, I suppose, who brought the sonnet into England: but, so far as I know, they did not write in the regular sonnet way, any of them. Was not Milton the first who did? I am not at all up in the subject, so if I have shewn lamentable ignorance of the history of the sonnet in these remarks, you must overlook it. What I mean is that English writers have seldom kept to the regular form: whether they had better have done so, is the question.

As to S. John Baptist.[1] I have always felt that the wildernefs was wrong: that it was a wild, not a sandy desert: but fear I cannot alter that now. There is a sandy desert of course to the south of Judæa. The Sons of the Unhappy I learned of from on[e] of Gibbon's notes. They were in a somewhat later time (not much) & I ventured to think that they were in the time of the Baptist. It seemed so striking a thing that there s^d be enough misery always to have a generation upon earth, & that this generation s^d always be. to be found in the Judaean desert.

I think 'The Other Mary'[1] not worth publishing: nor 'The Last Supper'.[1]

In the Addrefs,[1] what you say of the uncertainty of the variation of the refrain is very true: I must try something with it. In the stanza about 'labouring in the fatal wind &c.' would to *seek* a part make the metaphor better than to *have* a part?

Your notes on the tale about the Four Lovers are very valuable, especially on the metre, I think. So far as I remember the metre of Too Much Friendship is unsatisfactory and for the reason that you give, that it is a mixture of systems. There is also in both, I fear, a good deal of what one may call tagging. In fact I have never thoroughly pleased myself with a narrative or tale in verse. I shall however look at them again with the light that you throw.

In one letter you speak of Kingsley & the sort of corruption that he brought in: the bullying tone, the 'stand no blasted nonsense'. I know what you mean. It is a compound of bullying & Phariseeism, which has gone wide in the day's literature making, e.g. writers speak of their heroes bathing & sponging themselves in tubs of cold water: the insinuation being that people of other opinions were dirty. I have been wont to know it in my own mind long enough by the name of 'the stink': which I got from Swinburne, whom I heard read a bitter satire on one of the school named Ludlow, whom he compared to the

[1] If extant, in MS.

stink 'where[1] the Thames had laid the mud low', or something like that.[2] Happily it is going out. Henry Kingsley's books are entirely free from it, & excellent in tone, I think.

I think much of you, with an admiration that I cannot exprefs. But I will say no more now.

You told me of some musical airs.

Ever your affectionate Friend

                                           R. W. DIXON.

I ought to tell you that I am engaged to be married some time or other.

XXI

Manresa House, Roehampton, S.W. Oct. 29 1881.

MY DEAR FRIEND,—First I will bring to an end my criticisms on your poems; for I hear that our month's retreat is to begin on Wednesday evening. *Too Much Friendship*, though written with a flowing and a powerful pen, I find less pleasure in than in *Love's Casuistry*. The story has something of the primness of *Elegant Extracts* about it and this has infected the diction even.[3] The motive is good, the strain and its reaction, but between these two extremes the intermediate action has in it something, as Horace calls it, 'odiously incredible'. One feels, you must have felt, that Hypatia (whom Septimius could never have trusted: she would play the same trick after marriage) told her husband that Alcander was a *muff*, she had always felt it and his behaviour in the matter of the surrender made her certain; and that they were not grateful, on the contrary they could not forgive him the obligation he laid them under, looked sheepish when he turned up, and after his death without shame said that that was happiest for all concerned. The language is a quaint

   [1] Or 'when'.

   [2] Not in Swinburne's published works. Mr. T. J. Wise writes that he has found no trace of it among the poet's published or still unpublished writings or letters: nor did he ever hear Swinburne mention it.

   [3] The poem is based on *The Story of Alcander and Septimius* (Translated from a Byzantine historian), in *The Bee*, No. 1 (Saturday, October 6, 1759). There Alcander's excess of friendship in surrendering his bride to his friend Septimius has a 'happy ending'.

medley of Middle-Ages and 'QueenAnnery', a combination
quite of our age and almost even of our decade, as we see in
Morris and that school (to which you, I suppose, belong), and
having a charm of its own that I relish and admire, but as a
thing alien to me. Here is a pleasing instance:

> Rattled her keys, unfavourable sign,
> And on her turning wheel gan to decline.[1]

The first line is like the *Rape of the Lock*:

> Spadillio first, unconquerable lord—[2]

the second is like Spencer. It is the opening, I think, that
suffers most from Popery: one thinks it should have more
epigram or less of it. This spirit you throw off first at the fine
passage about the beasts in Spring.[3]

The other passages that strike me as finest are Septimius'
passionate cries and confession, especially at 'I cannot name
her';[4] Alcander's return from seeing the couple off in stormy
weather;[5] 'With him he long conferred . . . next he made';[6]
'There as he sat alone . . . car was seen', especially the stroke
about the clouds;[7] and Alcander's mad soliloquy.[8] The couplet
about the bat and dove is of canonical beauty[9] and the phrase
about 'the perfect pattern wretch',[10] besides of course many
scattered touches like 'walked when Hesper bid'.[11]

Alas! a fat lot of comfort the poor creature got from seeing
those two worldlings from St. John's Wood kneel over him, in
mortal dread that he would come to again.[12]

---

[1] This became ll. 250–4:
> Rattled her keys ('twas she indeed who thus,
> Combined with Love, upraised Septimius),
> And the same hour her favourite downwards thrust
> Upon that wheel that turns 'twixt cloud and dust.

[2] III. 49.   [3] ll. 105–16.   [4] ll. 162–72.   [5] ll. 247–58.
[6] ll. 489–92.   [7] ll. 507–14.   [8] ll. 544–59.
[9] ll. 199–200: Who that is set in strait 'twixt death and love
> But must refuse the bat and take the dove?
[10] l. 410.   [11] l. 346.
[12] A reference to the end of the poem: Septimius and Hypatia kneel beside the dying Alcander.

The passage about Rome 'Beside the Virgin's Fount . . . itself hath built' seems to me like taskwork and written in Castalian (which is a better name than Parnassian).[1]

I have now then nothing to do but to fold up your precious packet and return it, begging your pardon much for having kept it so long and expressing the pleasure the reading it has given me. The poems have grown on me while they have been in my keeping and would, I dare say, grow on me more if I read them longer, so that I feel that perhaps the objections I have made would fade away with a better appreciation and as my mind took from familiarity the right perspective of each thought as it came. On the beauties which characterise the whole I have spoken on different occasions in the course of criticising particulars and I do not like to repeat myself now. Their Muse still keeps the hold on my mind and affections it established many years ago. My mind indeed is older, its tastes undergo change, but then of course so is yours, and if I could not now be moved with such a fresh enthusiasm (I am not sure at least how it would be) as my almost boyhood was with the appletrees in *Mother and Daughter*, the nine lovers and their names and drapery in *Love's Consolation*, the march-past in *St. John*, the garland of images about the Church or the Beloved in the same, and many things in your first volume more, perhaps then I shd. not so well have appreciated the wind and wetness of your MS landscape pieces now by me. However this may be, richness of imagery belongs especially to youth, broader effects to the maturer mind; what therefore I now want to see is that great work, the epic or romance of which Bridges seemed to say great things, but the very subject of which I never learnt —And also those other pieces of which you spoke. But this cannot be just now, not till my time of tertianship is over. Of course they will not lose by keeping, if God spares your life. You shall therefore have the MS packet in a day or two after I send this.

As for my music, there are four tunes—(1) to 'the Feathers of the Willow' made years ago and only now extant in my

[1] ll. 350–60 in the printed version, which has evidently been shortened.

memory; (2) to *Sky that rollest ever*: my sister is harmonising this; she says she is doing her very best and as she likes it best of all the airs of mine she has seen it is likely she will make a good thing of it; and she is to send it straight to you, so that you may get it any day;[1] (3) to the *Rainbow*:[2] this is so very peculiar, that I cannot trust anyone to harmonise it and must, if the opportunity should offer and my knowledge ever be sufficient, do it myself; (4) to *Does the South Wind*:[3] this is not quite finished and only written in sol-fa score; it will wait too.

On the Sonnet and its history a learned book or two learned books have been published of late and all is known about it— but not by me. The reason why the sonnet has never been so effective or successful in England as in Italy I believe to be this: it is not so long as the Italian sonnet; it is not long enough, I will presently say how.[4] Now in the form of any work of art the intrinsic measurements, the proportions, that is, of the parts to one another and to the whole, are no doubt the principal point, but still the extrinsic measurements, the absolute quantity or size goes for something. Thus supposing in the Doric Order the Parthenon to be the standard of perfection, then if the columns of the Parthenon have so many semidiameters or modules to their height, the architrave so many, and so on these will be the typical proportions. But if a building is raised on a notably greater scale it will be found that these proportions for the columns and the rest are no longer satisfactory, so that one of two things—either the proportions must be changed or the Order abandoned. Now if the Italian sonnet is one of the most successful forms of composition known, as it is reckoned to be, its proportions, inward and outward, must be pretty near

---

[1] See Appendix III, 4 a.
[2] R. B. in his Notes (*S.P.*, p. 193) says: 'None of the others except *The Rainbow* poem was much praised by Hopkins. That poem cannot be found.' It seems evident that the poem later called, by G. M. H., *Fallen Rain* (*S.P.*, pp. 148–9) is referred to here as the *Rainbow*. See Appendix III, 4 c.
[3] *Ruffling Wind*, *S.P.*, p. 147.
[4] These remarks on the sonnet are of peculiar importance in view of G. M. H.'s practice.

perfection. The English sonnet has the same inward proportions, 14 lines, 5 feet to the line, and the rhymes and so on may
be made as in the strictest Italian type. Nevertheless it is notably
shorter and would therefore appear likely to be unsuccessful,
from want not of comparative but of absolute length. For take
any lines from an Italian sonnet, as

> Non ha l'ottimo⌢artista⌢alcun concetto
> Che⌢un marmor solo⌢in se non circonscriva.

Each line has two elisions and a heavy ending or 13 syllables,
though only 10 or, if you like, 11 count in the scanning. An
Italian heroic line then and consequently a sonnet will be longer
than an English in the proportion 13:10, which is considerable.
But this is not all: the syllables themselves are longer. We have
seldom such a delay in the voice as is given to the syllable by
doubled letters (as *ọttimo* and *conc̣etto*) or even by two or more
consonants (as *artịsta* and *c̣irconscriva*) of any sort, read as Italians
read. Perhaps then the proportions are nearer 4 : 3 or 3 : 2.
The English sonnet is then in comparison with the Italian short,
light, tripping, and trifling.

This has been instinctively felt and the best sonnets shew
various devices successfully employed to make up for the short-
coming. It may be done by the mere gravity of the thought,
which compels a longer dwelling on the words, as in Wordsworth (who otherwise is somewhat light in his versification), e.g.

> Earth has not anything to shew more fair—etc;

or by inversion and a periodic construction, which has something the same effect: there is a good deal of this in Bridges'
sonnets; or by breaks and pauses, as

> Captain or colonel or knight-ạt-arms;

or by many monosyllables, as

> Both them I serve and of their train am I:

this is common with τοὺς περὶ Swinburne;[1] or by the weight of
the syllables themselves, strong or circumflexed and so on, as

---

[1] 'Those around', or 'the followers of'.

may be remarked in Gray's sonnet, an exquisite piece of art, whatever Wordsworth may say,

> In vain to me the smiling mornings shine—

(this sonnet is remarkable for its falling or trochaic rhythm—

> In | vain to | me the | smiling | mornings | shine—

and not

> In vain | to me | the smil | ing morn | ings shine),

and it seems to me that for a mechanical difficulty the most mechanical remedy is the best: none, I think, meet it so well as these 'outriding' feet I sometimes myself employ, for they more than equal the Italian elisions and make the whole sonnet rather longer, if anything, than the Italian is. Alexandrine lines (used throughout) have the same effect: this of course is a departure from the Italian, but French sonnets are usually in Alexandrines.

The above reasoning wd. shew that any metre (in the same rhythm) will be longer in Italian than in English and this is in fact, I believe, the case and is the reason perhaps why the *ottava rima* has never had the success in England it has had in Italy and why Spencer found it necessary to lengthen it in the ration from 20 to 23 (= 80 to 92).

Surrey's sonnets are fine, but so far as I remember them they are strict in form. I look upon Surrey as a great writer and of the purest style. But he was an experimentalist, as you say, and all his experiments are not successful. I feel ashamed however to talk of English or any literature, of which I was always very ignorant and which I have ceased to read.

The alteration 'seek a part' will meet the difficulty of the mixed metaphor. 'Love's mast' will then be the post. But I had imagined that you were speaking of that mast itself as a place of danger, subject to the storms of speculation, panics, failures, inflations, depressions, 'bears', 'bulls', and swindles.

This must be my last letter on literary matters while I stay here, for they are quite out of keeping with my present duties. I am very glad my criticisms should be of any service to you: they have involved a labour of love.

Nov. 2—My sister is unwilling to send you the music, with which she is not satisfied, till I have seen it. It must therefore wait awhile.

I am ashamed at the expressions of high regard which your last letter and others have contained, kind and touching as they are, and do not know whether I ought to reply to them or not. This I say: my vocation puts before me a standard so high that a higher can be found nowhere else. The question then for me is not whether I am willing (if I may guess what is in your mind) to make a sacrifice of hopes of fame (let us suppose), but whether I am not to undergo a severe judgment from God for the lothness I have shewn in making it, for the reserves I may have in my heart made, for the backward glances I[1] have given with my hand upon the plough, for the waste of time the very compositions you admire may have caused and their preoccupation of the mind which belonged to more sacred or more binding duties, for the disquiet and the thoughts of vain-glory they have given rise to. A purpose may look smooth and perfect from without but be frayed and faltering from within. I have never wavered in my vocation, but I have not lived up to it. I destroyed the verse I had written when I entered the Society and meant to write no more; the *Deutschland* I began after a long interval at the chance suggestion of my superior, but that being done it is a question whether I did well to write anything else. However I shall, in my present mind, continue to compose, as occasion shall fairly allow, which I am afraid will be seldom and indeed for some years past has been scarcely ever, and let what I produce wait and take its chance; for a very spiritual man once told me that with things like composition the best sacrifice was not to destroy one's work but to leave it entirely to be disposed of by obedience. But I can scarcely fancy myself asking a superior to publish a volume of my verses and I own that humanly there is very little likelihood of that ever coming to pass. And to be sure if I chose to look at things on one side and not the other I could of course regret this

[1] Here 'may', cancelled.

bitterly. But there is more peace and it is the holier lot to be unknown than to be known.—In no case am I willing to write anything while in my present condition: the time is precious and will not return again and I know I shall not regret my forbearance. If I do get hereafter any opportunity of writing poetry I could find it in my heart to finish a tragedy of which I have a few dozen lines written and the leading thoughts for the rest in my head on the subject of St. Winefred's martyrdom: as it happens, tomorrow is her feastday.

I hope you may have all happiness in your marriage. You have, I think, no children of your own, but Bridges told me he met your two step daughters at Hayton.

I am afraid our retreat will not begin tonight after all.

Believe me always your affectionate friend

GERARD M. HOPKINS S.J.

I should tell you that my letters now are opened.

XXI A (Postcard)

The MSS. and the Music arrived safe. The Song is very beautiful: i.e. the music to which you have set it: very rare & delicate.

I have begun a letter to you: but have not time to finish it just now. Ever your affec^te Friend

R^d W. DIXON
11 Nov 1881

Hayton Vicarage
Carlisle

XXI B

Hayton Vicarage, Carlisle. 4 Nov. 1881.

MY DEAR, DEAR FRIEND,—Your Letter touches & moves me more than I can say. I ought not in your present circumstances tease you with the regret that much of it gives me: to hear of your having destroyed poems, & feeling that you have a vocation in comparison of which poetry & the fame that might assuredly be yours is nothing. I could say much, for my heart bleeds: but

I ought also to feel the same: and do not as I ought, though I thought myself very indifferent as to fame. So I will say nothing, but cling to the hope that you will find it consistent with all that you have undertaken to pursue poetry still, as occasion may serve: & that in so doing you may be sanctioned & encouraged by the great Society to which you belong, which has given so many ornaments to literature. Surely one vocation cannot destroy another: and such a Society as yours will not remain ignorant that you have such gifts as have seldom been given by God to man.

Another thing I have to say. I do not know whether you have fal[l]en in with what I have said about the Institution of your Society in my History:[1] but I have had a dread that you might be hurt thereby, if you happened to do so. I meant to be deeply respectful: but was, I think, liable to misunderstanding. If you have not, I hope you may not: but if you have, I hope you will see that I have tried not to be offensive, though I have been, as I think too free, & what may be called hoity toity. I hope to make amends, if I live long enough to come upon the period when I can do so.

Thank you for all you say of myself.

Now, as to your criticisms. I cannot enough thank you for them. They are entirely invaluable & I hope to profit by them. The remarks on the diction in that tale of Too Much Friendship are perfectly true: & I think that some of it must be altered. The instance you give is a glaring one: & I was wondering whether you would notice it: tho I did not know that there was so pat a parallel in Pope. I remember thinking it was of the *sort* as I wrote it. I rather wondered also whether you would observe anything on the piece about Hope, which is a sort of parallel to a pafsage in Ovid. I wish I had thought of the motives you give to Septimius & Hypatia: which w^d have given a far deeper moral significance. I did not discover till I had long finished the poem that the story is Goldsmith's. I found

---

[1] See NOTE I. R. W. D.'s words can have given no offence; they anticipate, at certain points, what G. M. H. himself says.

it in his Essays. If I had known that, I s^d have let it alone altogether. He makes it end happily: Alcander lives in Rome as
the friend of the other two & they reinstate him.

14 Nov.

I had written thus much ten days ago you see: & have thought
of tearing it up: but as it is written, & was written under great
& fresh feeling, I will let it go, though perhaps it may be
dissonant & jarring to you. I have since received and acknowledged the Packet & the Song. The latter my daughter has
played and sung: it seemed to me a very beautiful & appropriate melody: but I have no musical faculty. I judge of music
only by general taste. I can catch & remember airs very distinctly: but cannot judge of harmony, & have no notion of
composition. My Daughter thinks it not unlike some of Mr.
Metcalfe's settings.[1] This did not strike me: but, if so, Metcalfe
is a genius of very great scope: utterly unknown, and more or
lefs wasted, but a genius still. He was for years the only person
in Carlisle with whom I could exchange a word about art of
any sort. He is highly held by a few who know: among them
the late Dr. Wesley,[2] who wrote to him that he 'reverenced every
note that he had written'.

What you say of the English sonnet being absolutely shorter
than the Italian is very striking: it is so: and this may, as you say,
be the reason for so many English writers not adhering to the
Italian form. But if so, is it not a reason for my not adhering to
it. Or are my departures too licentious to be justified anyhow?
All that you say is really instructive. I do not however think
that Surrey's sonnets are regular: unlefs there be more than one
regular form in Italian. I understand by the regular form such as
Milton's & Bridges' = 2 identically rhymed quatrains set back to
back + sestet = 4 rhymes to 14 verses. Now Surrey has sonnets
with only 2 rhymes in them, others with 3: & other varieties.

---

[1] Evidently William Metcalfe, who, among other compositions, set various
poems to music (e.g. *Three Songs*—words by Tennyson, Kingsley, H. Coleridge—dedicated to the organist of Carlisle Cathedral, 1860).

[2] Samuel Sebastian Wesley (1810–76).

Another thing. I do not think I belong to the school of Morris. I have seen very little of his poetry: only three tales of the Earthly Paradise, & a little of Jason. Also that immense work Sigurd. So far as I can judge his touch is entirely different from mine: very powerful, even sledge-hammery: but not over subtle, by no means intellectual, and what I call desolately limited. His creed, that is, his ideas of life, is to me monstrous, & insupportable. His method, his mingling of the couplet measure & the old stanza in his tales—not mingling in the same tale, but using either one or the other—looks somehow like writing in ruins: gives a different imprefsion to what it gives when Chaucer does the same. His couplets in Jason, when I saw it last, seemed to have an immense deal of mere tagging. He very lawlefsly intersperses it with lyric songs, brought in in the midst of these couplets & interrupting it. I could no more do that than introduce a pafsage of prose: the one is as unjustifiable as the other. In short he has not (as I think) a high feeling for form. If he had, he would be a very great poet: which he just mifses being.

I shall, when time allows, go through my manuscripts with your letters in hand, & greatly improve them by the procefs. Perhaps I may write on some points. Do pardon me for interrupting you with these things but the time will surely come when I may.

Of Bridges I have not heard for some time. He was going abroad, but I do not know to what part of the world.

If you can let me have a letter at any not distant time, I shall be truly glad. Meantime I am your affectionate friend

R̤ W. Dixon

XXII

Manresa House, Roehampton, S.W. Dec. 1 1881

(the very day 300 years ago of Father Campion's martyrdom).

My dear friend,—I am heartily glad you did not make away with, as you say you thought of doing, so warm and precious a letter as your last. It reached me on the first break or day of repose in our month's retreat; I began answering it on the second, but could not finish; and this is the third and last of them.

When a man has given himself to God's service, when he has denied himself and followed Christ, he has fitted himself to receive and does receive from God a special guidance, a more particular providence. This guidance is conveyed partly by the action of other men, as his appointed superiors, and partly by direct lights and inspirations. If I wait for such guidance, through whatever channel conveyed, about anything, about my poetry for instance, I do more wisely in every way than if I try to serve my own seeming interests in the matter. Now if you value what I write, if I do myself, much more does our Lord. And if he chooses to avail himself of what I leave at his disposal he can do so with a felicity and with a success which I could never command. And if he does not, then two things follow; one that the reward I shall nevertheless receive from him will be all the greater; the other that then I shall know how much a thing contrary to his will and even to my own best interests I should have done if I had taken things into my own hands and forced on publication. This is my principle and this in the main has been my practice: leading the sort of life I do here it seems easy, but when one mixes with the world and meets on every side its secret solicitations, to live by faith is harder, is very hard; nevertheless by God's help I shall always do so.

Our Society values, as you say, and has contributed to literature, to culture; but only as a means to an end. Its history and its experience shew that literature proper, as poetry, has seldom been found to be to that end a very serviceable means. We have had for three centuries often the flower of the youth of a country in numbers enter our body: among these how many poets, how many artists of all sorts, there must have been! But there have been very few Jesuit poets and, where they have been, I believe it would be found on examination that there was something exceptional in their circumstances or, so to say, counterbalancing in their career. For genius attracts fame and individual fame St. Ignatius looked on as the most dangerous and dazzling of all attractions. There was a certain Fr. Beschi[1] who in Southern Hindustan composed an epic which has become one of the Tamul classics and is spoken of with unbounded admiration by those who can read it. But this was in India, far from home, and one can well understand that fame among Hindu pundits need not turn the head of an Italian. In England we had Fr. Southwell[2] a poet, a minor poet but still a poet; but he wrote amidst a terrible persecution and died a martyr, with circumstances of horrible barbarity: this is the counterpoise in his career. Then what a genius was Campion[3] himself! was not he a poet? perhaps a great one, if he had chosen. His History of Ireland, written in hiding and hurrying from place to place, Mr. Simpson in his Life[4] says, and the samples prove it, shews an eloquence like Shakspere's; and in fact Shakspere made use of the book. He had all and more than all the rhetoric of that golden age and was probably the most vigorous mind and eloquent tongue engaged in theological strife then in England, perhaps in Europe. It seems in time he might have done anything. But his eloquence died on the air, his genius was quenched in his blood after one year's employment in his country. Music is more professional than poetry perhaps and Jesuits have composed and well, but none has any fame to speak of. We had one painter who reached excellence, I forget his name, he was a

[1] Costanzo Giuseppe Beschi, whose *Tēm-bāv-ani* (an epic poem on the legends of St. Joseph and the Gospel narratives), with an interpretation by the author, and edited by the Abbé Dupuis, was published in 3 vols., 1851–3. Beschi was helped in writing this work by Supradīpa Kavi-rāyar.

[2] Robert Southwell (1561?–95).

[3] Edmund Campion's *A Historie of Ireland written in the Yeare 1571* (best read in *Ancient Irish Histories*, 1809, but printed before that by Holinshed in 1587 and Ware in 1633) is particularly interesting in those chapters (5 and 6) where the author is writing from his own observation of the manners and customs of the Irish, and is there a valuable complement to Spenser's *View*.

[4] *Edmund Campion. A Biography*, by Richard Simpson, 1867 (new ed. 1896); a well-documented study, evidently G. M. H.'s source of information for his projected poem on the martyr. There are interesting points of contact between the two men—e.g. Campion left Oxford for Dublin, where, in 1570, there was an abortive attempt to re-establish the ancient university.

laybrother; but then he only painted flower pieces.[1] You see then what is against me, but since, as Solomon says, there is a time for everything, there is nothing that does not some day come to be, it may be that the time will come for my verses. I remember, by the by, once taking up a little book of the life of St. Stanislaus[2] told or commented on under emblems; it was much in the style of Herbert and his school and about that date; it was by some Polish Jesuit. I was astonished at their beauty and brilliancy, but the author is quite obscure. Brilliancy does not suit us. Bourdaloue[3] is reckoned our greatest orator: he is severe in style. Suarez[4] is our most famous theologian: he is a man of vast volume of mind, but without originality or brilliancy; he treats everything satisfactorily, but you never remember a phrase of his, the manner is nothing. Molina[5] is the man who *made* our theology: he was a genius and even in his driest dialectic I have remarked a certain fervour like a poet's. But in the great controversy on the Aids of Grace, the most dangerous crisis, as I suppose, which our Society ever went through till its suppression, though it was from his book that it had arisen, he took, I think, little part. The same sort of thing may be noticed in our saints. St. Ignatius himself was certainly, every one who reads his life will allow, one of the most extraordinary men that ever lived; but after the establishment of the Order he lived in Rome so ordinary, so hidden a life, that when after his death they began to move in the process of his canonisation one of the Cardinals, who had known him in his later life and in that way only, said that he had never remarked anything in him

[1] David Zeghers (or Seghers or Segers), 1590–1661, painter of flowers, fruit, and garlands, became a Jesuit in 1614 and did much work for the colleges and chapels of his Order. See Bryan's *Dictionary of Painters and Engravers*. There is an example of his work at Dulwich.

[2] Stanislaus Kostka (1550–68), who became a Jesuit less than a year before he died, has been called 'a model and mirror of religious perfection'. He was canonized in 1726.

[3] Louis Bourdaloue (1632–1704), the great French preacher.

[4] Francisco Suarez (1548–1617), the founder of Suarism.

[5] Luis de Molina (1535–1600), perhaps the most learned and famous Jesuit theologian.

more than in any edifying priest. St. Stanislaus Kostka's life and vocation is a bright romance—till he entered the novice-ship, where after 10 months he died, and at the same time its interest ceases. Much the same may be said of St. Aloysius Gonzaga.[1] The Blessed John Berchmans[2] was beatified for his most exact observance of the rule; he said of himself and the text is famous among us, Common life is the greatest of my mortifications; Gregory XVI (I think) when the first steps were to be taken said of him too: At that rate you will have to canonize all the Roman College. I quote these cases to prove that show and brilliancy do not suit us, that we cultivate the common-place outwardly and wish the beauty of the king's daughter the soul to be from within.

I could say much more on all this, but it is enough and I must go on to other things. Our retreat ended on the 8th. The 'hoity toity' passage I have not seen; indeed I have never even had your book in my hands except one day when waiting to see Bridges in his sickness I found it on the table and was just going to open it—but to the best of my remembrance I did not then open it either. I have for some years past had to put aside serious study. It is true if I had been where your book was easy of access I should have looked at it, perhaps read it all, but in Liverpool I never once entered the public library. However if, as I hope, the time for reading history should ever come I shall try to read this one. You said once you did not pretend not to have a side and that you must write as an Anglican: this is of course and you could not honestly be an Anglican and not write as one. Do you know Cobbett's *Reformation*?[3] Cobbett was a most honest man but not an honest Anglican; I shd. rather say that he was an honest thinker and an honest speaker but not an honest actor-out of his convictions but is a con-

---

[1] A youth of great promise (1568–91); canonized in 1726.

[2] Remarkable for his fervent piety (1599–1621); canonized in 1888.

[3] 'A History of the Protestant Reformation in England and Ireland; showing how that event impoverished the main body of the people in those countries; . . . In a series of letters addressed to all sensible and just Englishmen' (1824–7).

spicuous 'bell in a bellcot' and 'signpost on a road'. The book is written with the greatest violence of language; I must own that to me the strength seems not at all too strong; but from the point of view of expediency it is far too much so, it has overshot its mark, and those for whom it is meant will not read it. I much wish some learned Catholic would reëdit it and bring it up to date.[1] The most valuable and striking part of it to me is the doctrine about the origin of pauperism:[2] I shd. much myself like to follow this out. My Liverpool and Glasgow experience laid upon my mind a conviction, a truly crushing conviction, of the misery of town life to the poor and more than to the poor, of the misery of the poor in general, of the degradation even of our race, of the hollowness of this century's civilisation: it made even life a burden to me to have daily thrust upon me the things I saw.

I have found to my dismay what I suspected before, that my sister only sent you the music to two stanzas of your Song, whereas I made it for six. How she came to make so dreadful an oversight I cannot tell: the music changes and she had remarked on the change. But I must get her to send the rest and then you will be able to judge of the whole. I do not believe that my airs —if I can compare them with the work of an accomplished musician—would really be found to be like Mr. Metcalf's— to judge by the two pieces of his that you sent me.

I should tell you that I by no means objected to the couplet 'Rattled her keys', I admired it as a happy medley: I thought the fusion or rather the pieing was less happy in the opening of the poem.

About sonnet-writing I never meant to override your own judgment. I have put the objections to licentious forms and I believe they hold. But though many sonnets in English may in point of form be great departures from and degenerations of the type, put aside the reference to the type, and they may in them-

---

[1] There is an abbreviated modern edition, revised, with notes and preface by Cardinal Gasquet.

[2] The 'beginning of pauperism' is mentioned in Letter IX, and dealt with at length in Letter XVI.

selves be fine poems of 14 lines. Still that fact, that the poet has tied himself within 14 lines and calls the piece a sonnet, lays him open to objection.

I must hold that you and Morris belong to one school, and that though you should neither of you have read a line of the other's. I suppose the same models, the same masters, the same tastes, the same keepings, above all, make the school. It will always be possible to find differences, marked differences, between original minds; it will be necessarily so. So the species in nature are essentially distinct, nevertheless they are grouped into genera: they have one form in common, mounted on that they have a form that differences them. I used to call it the school of Rossetti: it is in literature the school of the Praeraphaelites. Of course that phase is in part past, neither do these things admit of hard and fast lines; still consider yourself, that you know Rossetti and Burne Jones, Rossetti through his sympathy for you and Burne Jones—was it the same or your sympathy for him? This modern medieval school is descended from the Romantic school (Romantic is a bad word) of Keats, Leigh Hunt, Hood, indeed of Scott early in the century. That was one school; another was that of the Lake poets and also of Shelley and Landor; the third was the sentimental school, of Byron, Moore, Mrs. Hemans, and Haynes Bailey.[1] Schools are very difficult to class: the best guide, I think, are keepings. Keats' school chooses medieval keepings, not pure nor drawn from the middle ages direct but as brought down through that Elizabethan tradition of Shakspere and his contemporaries which died out in such men as Herbert and Herrick. They were also great realists and observers of nature. The Lake poets and all that school represent, as it seems to me, the mean or standard of English style and diction, which culminated in Milton but was never very continuous or vigorously transmitted, and in fact none of these men unless perhaps Landor were great masters of style, though their diction is generally pure, lucid, and unarchaic. They were faithful but not rich observers of nature.

[1] For 'Bayly'.

Their keepings are their weak point, a sort of colourless classical keepings: when Wordsworth wants to describe a city or a cloud-scape which reminds him of a city it is some ordinary rhetorical stage-effect of domes, palaces, and temples. Byron's school had a deep feeling but the most untrustworthy and barbarous eye, for nature; a diction markedly modern; and their keepings any gaud or a lot of Oriental rubbish. I suppose Crabbe to have been in form a descendant of the school of Pope with a strong and modern realistic eye; Rogers something between Pope's school and that of Wordsworth and Landor; and Campbell between this last and Byron's, with a good deal of Popery too, and a perfect master of style. Now since this time Tennyson and his school seem to me to have struck a mean or com-promise between Keats and the medievalists on the one hand and Wordsworth and the Lake School on the other (Tennyson has some jarring notes of Byron in *Lady Clare Vere de Vere*, *Locksley Hall* and elsewhere). The Lake School expires in Keble and Faber and Cardinal Newman. The Brownings may be reckoned to the Romantics. Swinburne is a strange pheno-menon: his poetry seems a powerful effort at establishing a new standard of poetical diction, of the rhetoric of poetry; but to waive every other objection it is essentially archaic, biblical a good deal, and so on: now that is a thing that can never last; a perfect style must be of its age. In virtue of this archaism and on other grounds he must rank with the medievalists.

This is a long ramble on literary matters, on which I did not want to enter.

At Torquay Bridges made at last a sudden and wonderful re-covery: so I am told, for he has not written. He then went abroad with a common friend of ours, Muirhead, and is, I suppose, likely to be abroad for the winter. And I am afraid when he returns I shall not see him; for I may now be called away at any time.

Earnestly thanking you for your kindness and wishing you all that is best I remain your affectionate friend

GERARD M. HOPKINS S.J.

Dec. 16 1881.

XXII A

Hayton Vicarage, Carlisle. 28 Jan. 1882

MY DEAR FRIEND,—This is intended not to be an answer to your last immensely valuable Letter: but an acknowledgment of the Song which I have received from your Sister: & also is written because I feel as if it were long since I wrote to you. The Song seems to me singularly beautiful & proper to the words: which words are too much honoured in being wedded to such music. I have the air running in my head. My daughters have been trying it many times over, & are charmed with it. I am making a copy of it for one of them who is away since it came. I cannot help, since I began this, taking up your last long letter to read again. As to the first part of it, in which you speak of your poetry, and its relation to your profession, I cannot but take courage to hope that the day will come, when so health-breathing and purely powerful a faculty as you have been gifted with may find its proper issue in the world. Bridges struck the truth long ago when he said to me that your poems more carried him out of himself than those of any one. I have again and again felt the same: & am certain that as a means of serving, I will not say your cause, but religion, you cannot have a more powerful instrument than your own verses. They have, of course with all possible differences of originality on both sides, the quality which Taine has marked in Milton: & which is more to be noted in his minor pieces than the great ones, of admiration—I forget Taine's expreſsion, but it means admiration (or in you other emotions also) which reaches its fulneſs & completeneſs in giving the exact aspect of the thing it takes: so that a peculiar contentation is felt.

To take another point in your letter, I have seen Cobbett's Reformation, indeed read a good deal of it. A great deal of it is true: the general view that the Reformation was not an admirable thing is true: but the reasons for which Cobbett thinks so are not very high: he thinks that the expediency of the Refn was inexpedient: was a mistake in calculation: or rather that no account was taken of public expediency in the haste of private expediency. He is an indignant utilitarian: nothing more: & his indignation has no other exprefsion than sheer abuse, which is wearisome in a while, unskilful & disgusting. What he says about pauperism is true enough.

Following yᵣ criticism (and also Bridges, who said much the same when he read it) I have much altered the beginning of Septimius & Alcander, and also cut away much of that grind of a description of Rome. But the most important thing I have done at it is to add six verses to the end, to deepen the moral; at the suggestion of something that you said. You may remember that it ended with Love handing back Alcander to Reason, so that he knew Septimius & Hypatia kneeling by him dying. I add¹

> They reasoned too: as on his death they gazed,
>
> One hideous $\genfrac{}{}{0pt}{}{\text{common}}{\text{mutual}}$ thought their bosoms raised,
>
> Which out of being smote the only good
> That he had gained in all—their gratitude.
> 'So is it best for us,' Septimius said:
> Hypatia looked, and nodded o'er the dead.

I sᵈ like to have yᵣ opinion on this.

Your classification of the modern poet schools seems to me to hold: & especially I like what you say of Wordsworth. But I must now stop.

Ever your affectionate Friend

R. W. Dixon

XXIII

Manresa House, Roehampton, S.W. Feb. 1 1882.

My dear Friend,—I was almost writing to you when your letter came. I am now very busy; for, after taking some duty at Preston (St. Ignatius's) from the First Sunday in Lent, I am to go to Maryport in Cumberland to help in mission-services to

---

¹ The end suggested here is not that of the printed version. The main difference is in the second line above, which should take the place of:
Love sent one thought that both their bosoms raised.

be carried on there for the fortnight before Palm Sunday: I am therefore at work preparing instructions and other discourses. I should return here after that unless countermanded.

I do certainly think that the added lines to *Too Much Friend-ship* throw a vein of much deeper pathos and interest back through the whole story. I should like however the 4th of them to end with '—gratitude', omitting 'their', as more crisp and pointed—something like

'That all that grief had earned him—gratitude.'
I think also that Septimius should speak either more reservedly without *us*, as:

' "It was the best to be" Septimius said'—
or else more cynically, something like:

' "He rests—and we may rest" Septimius said'.[1]
I would remark that you have made Septimius of beautiful character and worthy of being Alcander's friend early in the story, but from the moment when he 'refused the bat and chose the dove', which though it was not selfish was far from being unselfish (if I may speak so illogically), he may be supposed to have declined and Hypatia to have corrupted him. About her there is no difficulty and the situation itself puts her in a more odious light.

My mind is much employed at present on the subject of Sacrifice, about which I am getting together some materials, with a view possibly to write about it some day: I do not know of course but I fancy it may be the case that nothing at all exhaustive or satisfactory has been written on it either specu-latively or historically. Something my brother, who is a Chinese scholar, furnished me the other day reminded me of two lines in an early poem of yours. A certain pious and devoted prince of early times called T'ang offered himself as a propitiatory sacri-fice in a great drought for the sake of his people. He went 'in a plain carriage, drawn by white horses, *clad in rushes, in the guise of a sacrificial victim,* . . . to a forest of mulberry trees, and there

---

[1] These suggestions are not adopted in the version printed.

prayed'. Now was it a fancy or was it following some tradition
that made you say:

> I took weak waterweeds to fold
> About my sacrificial dress—?[1]

and if the latter what?

Bridges has been writing to me from Florence about your
poem of 'Mano' and says that 'it is a marvellous work, full of
the richest things, and quite unlike anything else', but that he
has not room to describe it, with more, all of which makes me
of course eager to see it; but that cannot be yet.

I should not have thought that Cobbett was merely a utilitarian. His seemingly heartfelt remarks about love of country
for instance (I mean patriotism) and its dependence on beauty
of buildings and historic monuments are those of a man who has
other ideals than utility.

I am very glad indeed you are so well pleased with the music.
I shall hope to send you one or two more of your pieces some day.
My sister tells me she has had from you a very flattering letter.

The winter has been so mild with us that primroses have
been in bloom in our shrubberies for three weeks or so.

Believe me your affectionate friend

GERARD HOPKINS S.J.

Feb. 3 1882.

XXIV

Our Lady and St. Patrick's, Maryport. March 26 1882.

MY DEAR FRIEND,—I mean to be at Carlisle tomorrow by the
train which reaches there at 12.25 and to leave it for Preston
at about 4: could I hope to meet you? If not I can employ
myself at the Cathedral and otherwise of course. The chance
may never occur again.

Believe me yours affectionately

GERARD HOPKINS S.J.

If you missed me at the station you might find me at the
Cathedral perhaps. ·

[1] *C.C.*, *Dream*, p. 58, ll. 9–10.

103

XXV

St. Wilfrid's, Preston. Palm Sunday [2 April] 1882

My dear Friend,—I am still lingering at Preston, expecting to go south tomorrow or next day. I was detained here and closely employed, or I shd. have dropped you a line before to thank you, which I never did, for your kind entertainment at Carlisle.

I wish our meeting cd. have been longer for several reasons, but to name one, I fancied you were shy and that time would have been needed for this to wear off. I think that for myself I have very little shyness left in me, but I cannot communicate my own feeling to another.

I have nothing more to say now, but when I see anything settled you shall hear. In the meantime as long as I am at Roehampton, at least in the character of a novice, I do not ask to see *Mano* or anything important of yours—which nevertheless, in MS or print, I do of course earnestly hope to see.

Believe me your affectionate friend

GERARD M. HOPKINS S.J.

XXV A

Hayton, Carlisle. 13 Ap. 1882

My dear Friend,—I ought to have written before: but things have been in the way: to say how very glad I am to have seen you & to have a full knowledge what you are like. So far as I can remember, you are very like the boy of Highgate. I dare say I seemed 'shy': I have an unfortunate manner: & am constantly told that I am too quiet: I have often tried to overcome it: but the effort is always apparent to those with whom I am, & never succeeds. You must therefore forgive it: it is not from want of feeling or affection.

I feel the death of Rofsetti most acutely.[1] I have known him for twenty years: he was one of my dearest friends, though I

[1] He died 10 April 1882.

only saw much of him at one period, & that not a long one. It leaves an awful blank.

I am now called out, so good bye: wishing you every poſsible happineſs, & among others that you may soon be at liberty to write, & may write poems.

I am My dear Friend Ever your affec.ᵗⁱᵉ

R. W. Dixon

XXV B¹

Hayton Vicarage Carlisle. 15 Dec. 1882

My dear Friend,—I have been longer in answering you than I intended from the gladneſs that it was to me to see your hand-writing again. I am very glad to hear that you are employed in some teaching & literary work, even though it may not be exactly of the kind that I at least should be able by acquirements to be able to judge of. My own experience is that any teaching, any literary work is good for the mind provided that it be literary, by which I include philosophy & exclude mathematics. I hear from Bridges that you have sent him a 'very fine' poem:² wh. is excellent news. You speak of Mano.³ I am revising him from Bridges's suggestions: & find it rather a toil: I only give off days to it. I have not quite reached the end of Book 1. Bridges likes it, & has taken vast pains about it. Nearly everything he says is right. I am also going on with my Church History: & am in the middle of the year 1551.

Rossetti's death is a very sad thing indeed. Hall Caine's book⁴ contains a short contribution from me, at his request, to say what R.'s share in the Oxford & Cambridge Magazine was, & gives one or two other recollections. I agree with much of what you say of Rossetti. He was a man of extraordinary gifts: who

---

¹ In answer to a letter that has disappeared. G. M. H. was now at Stonyhurst.

² Perhaps *The Leaden Echo and the Golden Echo*, *Poems*, 36.

³ Published in 1883.

⁴ *Recollections of Dante Gabriel Rossetti*, by T. Hall Caine, 1882. R. W. D.'s contribution (pp. 36–40) is of particular interest. It was he who suggested starting the *Oxford and Cambridge Magazine*.

105

rose at once, very early, to a great development, & then stood still, through some lack. He has however made a mark.

I have heard a good deal from Bridges lately: mostly concerning Mano. His Prometheus seems to me a very good poem: particularly the choruses: extremely Greek in feeling. The difficulty seems to me the impossible state of things, without fire, what the story supposes.

As to Tennyson's Promise of May:[1] I should suppose that it failed from want of interest, though I speak only on hearsay. It seems to have had no plot: or only a slight single plot, & a wretched lot of characters: & to have been written in prose. How Tennyson could waste his time in writing a thing of that sort is a greater wonder than that it should fail. The only thing he could do for the drama w^d be to try to reform it; but that w^d not be by writing in prose the adventure of the cold blooded sort of being that might have figured in one of the Nineteenth Century Magazine's 'Symposiums'. At present the sooner the lingering falsity is got rid of that the acted drama is in any way an exhibition of noble pafsion, or a vehicle of wit, fancy, imagination, or good writing, the better. Let it be frankly acknowledged to be what it is, without the slightest pretence to be anything else: viz. a paradise of basenefs & folly, merely jolly and idiotic: but of art an extinct kind: having lefs to do with poetry than waxworks have.

Tennyson's Queen Mary (the best I suppose of his 'dramatic works') shewed very little ability of any sort. There was no dramatic knowledge: but that was not to be expected: but there was no dramatic *tone*: no go, no vigour. The speeches were all about five lines long, & hooked on to one another in the way of direct reply mostly: & these unsatisfactory morsels were interspersed with monstrous sermons, three pages long! And the incidents that were *related* (not acted) instead of being

---

[1] *The Promise of May* (which most deservedly failed on the stage) was included in the volume, *Locksley Hall Sixty Years After* (1886). There is a long review of this book in the *Athenaeum* of 1 Jan. 1887, and another, written by H. C. Beeching, in the *Academy* of the same date.

brought in with force, or at least conversationally, were brought
in in the way of 'making a statement'. I send you a Photograph,
asking for one in return.

Ever your affectᵉ friend

R. W. DIXON

XXVI¹

This private printing of *Prometheus*² may turn out unfortunate.
I have myself no taste for what is called dainty in the get up of
books and am altogether wanting in the spirit of a bookhunter.
10s. seems like what is called a prohibitive price. I could not
recommend our library to get such a book and till the second
edition I shall not see the poem in print.

I do not so strongly feel the objection about the fireless state
supposed. Some of the people of New Guinea were lately for
some time, a generation perhaps, without fire: they were very
wretched and a disease of the gums spread among them, still
they lived. Perhaps you mean that the poem makes the fire
not only wanting in fact but even unprocurable from nature.
But it is agreed that it is very hard to raise it and one may make,
in favour of the myth, some allowance for a malignant providence
which always easily baffled men's efforts in that direction.

Is it not an objection or do you avail yourself of the fact, that
Mano means Hand? Perhaps I might shortly, say at Easter,
if it were convenient to you, see at least some portion of it.

Believe me your affectionate friend

GERARD HOPKINS S.J.

Feb. 9 1883.

XXVII

Stonyhurst, Blackburn. June 25 1883.

MY DEAR FRIEND,—I am ashamed to think how long I have
let you go unanswered: it was bitter winter weather, I remember
you said, when you wrote; but the winter was very late this
year. It came March 20.

¹ The first part of this letter is missing.
² Privately printed by H. Daniel, in an edition of 100 copies, in this year.

I have little to say. I enclose one sonnet,[1] meant as a companion to one beginning 'I remember a house',[2] which perhaps you have. You will see that the first words begin a lyric of yours—or perhaps those are 'Earth, *sad* Earth'.[3] During May I was asked to write something in honour of the Blessed Virgin, it being the custom to hang up verse-compositions 'in the tongues' (which sometimes are far fetched, for people gravitate to us from odd quarters): I did a piece[4] in the same metre as 'Blue in the mists all day',[5] but I have not leisure to copy it.

Both your new poem and Bridges' linger.

We have duly got your History, but till holiday time I shall not look at it. Reading history is very laborious to me: I can only digest or remember a little at a time.

My time, as I have said before this, is not so closely employed but that someone else in my place might not do a good deal, but I cannot, and I see no grounded prospect of my ever doing

---

[1] *Ribblesdale*

'Vanitati enim creatura subjecta est, non volens sed propter eum qui subjecit eam in spe' cum praecc. et sqq. Rom. viii 20.

> Earth, sweet Earth, sweet landscape with leavès throng
> And louchèd low grass, heaven that dost appeal
> To, with no tongue to plead, no heart to feel,
> That canst but only be, but dost that long.
> Thou canst but be, but that thou well dost; strong
> Thy plea with him who dealt, nay does now deal
> Thy lovely dale down thus and thus lets reel
> Thy river and o'er gives all to rack or wrong.
> But what is Earth's eye, tongue, or heart else, where
> Else, but in dear and doggèd man?—Ah, the heir,
> To his own self-bent so bound, so tied to his turn,
> To thriftless reave both our rich round world bare
> And none reck of world after—this bids wear
> Earth brows of such care, care and dear concern.

Stonyhurst 1883

[2] *Poems*, 16.
[3] The lyric *Mercy* from *H.O.* (*S.P.*, p. 59), beginning:
> Earth, sad earth, thou roamest
> Through the day and night.
[4] *Poems*, 37.
[5] *Nature and Man*: the sixth of *Lyrical Poems* (*S.P.*, pp. 116–20).

much not only in poetry but in anything at all. At times I do feel this sadly and bitterly, but it is God's will and though no change that I can foresee will happen yet perhaps some may that I do not foresee.—I fumble a little at music, at counterpoint, of which in course of time I shall come to know something; for this, like every other study, after some drudgery yields up its secrets, which seem inpenetrable at first. If I could get to accompany my own airs I should, so to say, enter into a new kingdom at once, for I have plenty of tunes ready.

Your health is, I hope, good, for when you wrote you were suffering greatly from the cold. We have had drought in Lancashire, a rare thing: now the fine weather is broken up and there is much rain.

In the sonnet enclosed 'louchéd' is a coinage of mine and is to mean much the same as *slouched, slouching.* And I mean 'throng' for an adjective as we use it here in Lancashire.

This is but a scrub of a letter, but I could not make it longer or better now.

Believe me your affectionate friend

GERARD M. HOPKINS S.J.

June 28 1883.

June 29—I mislaid this under books yesterday and it was not posted—I suppose that I might light upon this, as I have this very minute—*Athenaeum* for June 9 'Literary Gossip[1] . . . Canon Dixon's new poem, entitled "Mano: a Poetical History", is written in *terza rima*, the measure being treated more upon structural principles than it has generally been in English. The time is the close of the tenth century, when there was a general expectation of the end of the world. The hero is a Norman knight, a precursor of the Normans who conquered Italy and Sicily in the next century, and the scenes are laid partly in Normandy, partly in Italy. The famous Gerbert, who became Pope and was a reputed magician, is among the characters.'

[1] G. M. H. gives the whole note.

XXVII A

Hayton Vicarage, Carlisle. 12 Aug. 1883

MY DEAR FRIEND,—I have left your last kind & interesting letter too long unanswered: & now I am not, I feel, in spirits to answer it: but I have a little time on hand, & you have been, & are, much in my thoughts: therefore I write, but having little to say.

I like the Sonnet on Earth the Creature, which you sent, very much, as I do all your work: it has the rarenefs, the sweetnefs that is in all: & could have been written by none other. Of the other poem which you mention, on Our Lady, it is probably the same that Bridges has mentioned to me, saying that it is 'admirable', 'Our Lady compared to the Air we breathe'.

Thank you very much for copying that notice of my poem from the Athenæum. The book is out, & I hope to send you a copy in a day or two. I want your judgment of it.

Bridges' poem came to me two days ago. It reads splendidly, especially the choruses: & (what is I s^{d} think extremely difficult) the verse for verse dialogue. He has managed the plot also excellently. By the way, what do you understand by 'unity of action'? The phrase is used by Hall Caine in a good article on Shakespeare in the Contemporary[1] in a way that I do not understand of it. I forget his exact words, something like the end being harmonious with the inception. I thought it meant having a single plot. Greek dramas have a single plot.

I have been reading over some of poor Rossetti's work. There is something very grieving in most of it. I thought, though it must seem presumptuous, that many of the sonnets might have been improved.

I wish the present run, or rather rush, upon the Sonnet were over. It is a bore to see the inevitable 'regular structure' week after week in all the 'cultured' organs, the fifth verse for ever virtuously turning the others, as it were, inside out. But I must not reopen the subject with you, to bore you.

---

[1] For June 1883 (pp. 883–900), *Two Aspects of Shakespeare's Art.*

Do you happen to know Rowe's Lucan?[1] It seems to me the finest version made in that age: the versification far better than Dryden, & more of a direct advance from him than Pope, which was rather another kind (I think) than an advance on Dryden.

Thank you for procuring my Church History: I hope if you read it, that there may be nothing to offend you. I trust not. I am going on with it, & am in the year 1551, a dreadful time.

With all good wishes and affectionate regards, I am
ever your affectionate Friend

R. W. DIXON

XXVIII

The Holy Name, Oxford Rd., Manchester. Aug. 12 1883.

MY DEAR FRIEND,—I am here filling a gap and take the opportunity of letting you know that two days before our 'Great Academies', that is the speechday with which our Stonyhurst scholastic year ends, Coventry Patmore came to visit us and stayed three or four days. The Rector gave me charge of him and I saw a good deal of him and had a good deal of talk. He knew and expressed great admiration of Bridges' Muse upon the strength of extracts in reviews only, not having till that time been able to get the poems from his bookseller; but of you he knew nothing, not even your name. I brought him all I had of yours in MS and he read it all. He told me he was very slow in taking in a new poet, even the meaning, much more the effect and spirit; he said 'I feel myself[2] in presence of a new mind, a new spirit, but beyond that at a first reading I am not yet accustomed to the strange atmosphere'. This he said after a little reading of the MS. Then he became much taken up with *Love's Consolation* and that made the most impression. He was in fact completely won by it and pointed out passages with the insight of the predestined reader. In the end he told me when I next wrote to you to express to you 'the immense pleasure the

[1] First published in 1718.
[2] MS. 'oneself'. G. M. H. has written 'I' above 'One', cancelled, but forgot to make the necessary change here.

reading of your poems had given him'; he was amazed and sorry he had never known anything of them before. I furnished him with titles and publisher and told him to expect *Mano*'s coming out. He would have it that Morris must have borrowed from you, but I told him I thought that it was a case of parallel growth. His conversation was of course full of interest. He is fastidious and searching in his criticism. Of his friend Aubrey de Vere he said, assenting to a remark of mine, 'He has all the gifts that make a poet excepting only that last degree of individuality which is the most essential of all'. Of Browning, whom he can no longer bring himself to read, he said something the same but severer. I suppose I am more tolerant or more inclined to admire than he is, but in listening to him I had that malignant satisfaction which lies in hearing one's worst surmises confirmed—the joy Mrs. Candour's audience must have felt when she discussed Mrs. Vermilion and Miss Evergreen.[1]

I expect on Thursday to go to my father's at Hampstead and in a week's time to Holland for a week. I suppose I shall be back at Stonyhurst by the beginning of next month. I am reappointed for the ensuing year, I am happy to say.

Believe me your affectionate friend

GERARD HOPKINS S.J.

I shall see Bridges at Hampstead, I expect.

By the by Patmore has a very great admiration for Dorset Barnes.

XXIX

The Holy Name, Oxford Road, Manchester. Aug. 15 1883.

MY DEAR FRIEND,—Your letter was brought me from Stony-hurst by hand yesterday and your book came by parcel post today: for both I heartily thank you. I have nearly finished the first Book, but at a first reading it would be too soon to speak.

---

[1] Sheridan, *The School for Scandal*, Act II, sc. ii. It should be 'Miss Vermillion' and 'Mrs. Evergreen'.

The style is more consistently archaic than I had expected: this style easily lends itself to pathetic effects but not so easily to powerful ones. A pageant of beauties passes before my mind as I read, but, much as Mr. Patmore said, I need time and re-reading to take the effect fairly in. So I will wait a while before writing further.

By 'unity of action' I understand (but I am not advised of the subject) not simplicity of plot (in the ordinary sense of simple, that is the opposite of complex) but connectedness of plot. There is unity of action, as I understand, if the plot turns on one event, incident, or, to speak more technically, motive and all its parts and details bear on that and are relevant to that: if they are irrelevant or disconnected or involve by-issues then the unity of action is impaired. So I have been accustomed to understand the phrase. The plot in some Greek plays is simple, slight, in the extreme: the *Agamemnon* for instance is what we should call rather a scene than a plot, a scene leading up to and then leading off from one incident, the hero's murder; but the unity of action is also extreme, for almost every word said and thing done leads up to, turns on, influences, or is influenced by this. But in this play there is also the 'unity of place' and, by a conventional abridgment, the semblance of 'unity of time'. Where, as in the *Eumenides*, these two unities are not observed the plot becomes more complicated. The plot, quite in our modern sense of plot, is well enough marked in the *Oedipus King* though the unities of time and place are there observed. In general I take it that other things being alike unity of action is higher the more complex the plot; it is the more difficult to effect and therefore the more valuable when effected. We judge so of everything. In practice something must be sacrificed, and on what shall be sacrificed temperaments differ and discover their differences. The incidents for instance of Goethe's *Faust* are fascinating, but the unity of action, the bearing of all these on one common lesson the play is to teach or effect it is to produce, is not telling at first sight and is perhaps—I have no opinion—really defective. The Gk. dramas are on the other hand well concentrated, but the play of incident and character is often slight: one does not quote from them either stage-effects or types of character. But my thoughts are unverified and undigested.

A friend recommended me if I met with them to read L. Stevenson's stories, the *New Arabian Nights*[1] and others since. I read a story by him in *Longman's*, I think, and a paper by him on Romance.[2] His doctrine, if I apprehend him, is something like this. The essence of Romance is incident and that only, the type of pure Romance the *Arabian Nights:* those stories have no moral, no character-drawing, they turn altogether on interesting incident. The incidents must of[3] course have a connection, but it need be nothing more than that they happen to the same person, are aggravations and so on. As history consists essentially of events likely or unlikely, consequences of causes chronicled before or what may be called chance, just retributions or nothing of the sort, so Romance, which is fictitious history, consists of event, of incident. His own stories are written on this principle: they are very good and he has all the gifts a writer of fiction should have, including those he holds unessential, as characterisation, and at first you notice no more than an ordinary well told story, but on looking back in the light of this doctrine you see that the persons illustrate the incident or strain of incidents, the plot, *the story*, not the story and incidents the persons. There was a tale of his called the *Treasure of Fourvières*[4] or something like that; it is the story of an old treasure found, lost, and found again. The finding of the treasure acts of course and rather for the worse upon the finder, a retired French doctor, and his wife; the loss cures them; you wait to see the effect of the refinding: but not at all, the story abruptly ends—because its hero was, so to say, this triplet of

---

[1] Published in 1882 (reviewed in the *Athenaeum* of 12 Aug.).

[2] 'A Gossip on Romance', *Longman's Magazine*, Nov. 1882, pp. 69–79. Reprinted in *Memories and Portraits*, 1887.

[3] MS. 'have'.

[4] 'The Treasure of Franchard', *Longman's Magazine*, April and May, 1883. Reprinted in *The Merry Men*, 1887.

incidents. His own remarks on the strength and weakness of the Waverleys are excellent. But I have been giving my own version of the doctrine (which is, I think, clearly true) rather than his for I do not remember well enough what he says.

Now I think Shakspere's drama is more in this sense romantic than the Greek and that if the unity of action is not so marked (as it is not) the *interest of romance*, arising from a well calculated strain of incidents, is greater. You remember the scene or episode of the little Indian boy in the *Midsummer Night*: it is, I think, an allegory, to which, in writing once on the play, I believed I had found the clue, but whether I was right or wrong the meaning must have in any case been, and Shakspere must have known it wd. be, dark or invisible to most beholders or readers; yet he let it stand, just, as I suppose, because it is interesting as an incident in the story, not that it throws any light on the main plot or helps the unity of action, but rather, at all events superficially, hinders it. I could write much more but must stop. I am shortly starting for London, where my address is Oak Hill, Hampstead, N.W. I am going to let Mr. Patmore know *Mano* is out: I heard from him this morning.

Believe me gratefully and affectionately your friend

GERARD HOPKINS S.J.

Aug. 16.

XXIX A

Hayton Vicarage, Carlisle. 24 Aug. 1883.

MY DEAR FRIEND,—I write a line in haste to thank you for your immensely interesting Letter. Your remarks on Unity of action are, I think, the truth: i.e. that so far from that being the same thing as singlenefs of plot, it may be most perfect in a plot complicated with incidents, or a mixture of two or three plots or stories: as in, e.g. the Merchant of Venice, where you have the story of the Merchant & Jew, that of the Caskets, & that (a very slight one) of Lorenzo & Jessica. But still, as a fact, the Greek plays, out of wh. the Unity was evolved as a law of the drama, have only one plot or story. I conclude that

Shakespeare held that unity might be preserved—essential unity—while complications & mixture of plots might be admitted, & as you say, increase the value of the unity, ultimately preserved, by the difficulty added, and even by the apparent breach of unity.

I have nothing to write but this acknowledgement: and therewith to thank you very warmly for interesting Mr. Patmore in my poems. He sends me a message through you in your last letter. Please thank him, whenever you write. I read part of the Angel in the House very long ago, & remember being pleased especially with a description of a 'stony-built sky'. I am not sure of the exactness of my memory of the phrase: but it was a very forcibly life-like one.

I hope you may enjoy your trip to Holland: a land that I have desired with desire to see.

Ever your affectionate friend

R. W. DIXON.

XXX

Stonyhurst, Blackburn. Oct. 11 1883.

MY DEAR FRIEND,—This is not a proper letter but a line or so to say more shall be presently forthcoming with remarks on *Mano.* I took the book abroad with me, read it once cursorily, then began a more careful study, but this I interrupted on my return, for there was something pressing in the way of poetical criticism I had promised to do,[1] and in the meantime I lent it to one of my pupils, who has it now.

On the second reading the great beauty of the verse came out. I also found the archaism of the diction did not stand in the way of powerful effects, but allowed of vigorous and homely language, as in the line about the pull at the Roman rope. Of imagery the beauties were countless. (What I am saying now is a mere gabble.) The story is tragic in the extreme. My present puzzle

---

[1] His detailed criticism of *The Angel in the House* which Patmore used in a new edition of the poem.

116

is that I cannot find the clew to it. Mano seems some sort of type of man; an Adam, betrayed by an Eve. Gerbert seems something of a serpent. I never cd. get out of my head that *he* was the 'valley-wight': if there is nothing in this you may be sure others will think so nevertheless. I could not interpret the dream of the rabbits, lovely as it is. I cannot be reconciled to Mano's killing Joanna: I do not see that he could be justified, terrible as the occasion was. Nor can I understand his falling away on the journey to Italy. Pathos and strokes of the human heart abound throughout; the scene where Mano visits Blanche and her husband disguised comes back to me as particularly lovely in this respect; but I will write no more remarks of my own till I get the book back. I shall now tell you what Mr. Patmore says.

Mano, he writes, 'is full of vigour and manly and even great style; but I think that a reader, alert, as I am, to watch for indications of the inner motive of the poem, ought to be enabled to discover it more clearly than I am as yet able to do'. This seems to be my own difficulty. But more hereafter.

There has been and will be no time for my reading your history.

Believe me your affectionate friend

GERARD HOPKINS S.J.

Oct. 14 1883.

I have again missed the post.

XXX A

Hayton Vicarage, Carlisle. 19 Nov. 1883

MY DEAR FRIEND,—I have kept you so long without answer, that I feel it impossible not to write now, though for aught I have to say I might have written long since.

Your opinion of Mano is not so favourable as I wish: & I do not know how to meet your main objection: but so far as I can judge myself, there should be a central motive in faith (in its human aspect fidelity) struggling with fate or accident & mis-understanding. I fear that this is not made apparent enough, since both you & Mr. Patmore have felt the same lack of some-thing. With regard to Mano's conduct in the last scene, your objection never occurred to me. Perhaps you are right.

To turn to something else. I have lately written an account of Ireland in the reign of Edward vi for the third volume of my Church History. Do you happen to have any records of your Society at Stonyhurst bearing on that period? There were some Missionaries there who were spoken of by Archb. Browne of Dublin in a sermon in 1551 or 1552. And there was a blind bishop, often called 'the blind Scot' in State Papers, whose name was Waucop, Lat. Venantius, who was provided to Armagh when Cromer died, about 1542. He was a doctor of Paris, present at Trent, and a remarkable man. He had a good deal to do with your Society, & I think lived in it at Paris at one time. I believe he died in Ireland about 1551.

You may possibly have heard from Bridges that I am about to leave Hayton for Warkworth, in Northumberland: to which the Bishop of Carlisle has presented me. I suppose I shall be there before Christmas.

Do not take any trouble about the records. There are the names of some early members of your Order, who were in Ireland at that time, in one of the histories that I have here. They seem Spanish or Italian names. If nothing particular is known, I would not add to what I have said. But the history of the Society altogether in these isles is very little known: & I hope, as I go on, to do some sort of justice to its heroic devotion, even if the cause be not wholly my own.

I see, on looking at your letter again, that your judgment is not fully settled on Mano. What you say in praise of it is very gratifying. Can you send me anything of your own? Bridges has spoken of some not long since done.

       I am ever

          Your affectionate Friend

                 R. W. Dixon

XXXI

University College. 85 & 86, Stephen's Green. Dublin.
March 25 1884

MY DEAR FRIEND,—In writing last (and I hope you got that letter: it was addressed to Hayton and contained my riper thoughts of *Mano*)[1] I forgot to reply to some things you had spoken of.

The two Jesuits in Ireland were Frs. Paschasius Brouet or Broet and Alphonsus Salmeron, both of St. Ignatius's first companions.[2] Their mission to Ireland is well known, but it wd. be interesting to hear of it from the Government side. About the Blind Scot I consulted Fr. Wm. Forbes-Leith. He is a learned and indefatigable historian and antiquary and it wd. even be well for you on such points to apply to him, for on that period and in the matter of Scotch Catholics in particular he has an unflagging interest and first hand knowledge. He went quite lately to Simancas to 'research'. He has written a history of the Scotch Guard at the French court, edited Turgot's Life of Queen Margaret of Scotland, and is now busy on the annals of the Scotch Jesuits.[3] He never lets a minute go idle and after his teaching-work at once returns to his own studies. He is to be found at Stonyhurst. He knew all about the Blind Scot, but what he told me, if he told me anything particular, I have forgotten. But if necessary you can write and hear from himself.

Believe me your affectionate friend

GERARD M. HOPKINS S.J.

[1] This letter, which should fill so essential a place in the correspondence, is missing.

[2] Alphonsus Salmeron (1515–85), a Jesuit biblical scholar whose chief writings are commentaries on the Scriptures was, in 1541, sent by Paul III with Pascase Broët (1500–62), as joint apostolic nuncio to Ireland. They landed on 23 Feb. 1542, and thirty-four days later they set sail for Dieppe on the way to Paris.

[3] *Narratives of Scottish Catholics under Mary Stuart and James VI* (1885); add also *The Life of Saint Cuthbert* (1888).

XXXI A

Warkworth Vicarage, Northumberland. April 14 1884.

MY DEAR FRIEND,—I have been long in answering your Letters: and yet I take the first opportunity. I cannot say how glad I am to have your full judgment on Mano. There must be some difficulty about the poem at first sight, which may account for the various opinions of those who have written of it. It is a relief to me that it gains on you: what you say of the diction and imagery is extremely satisfactory, and gave me great pleasure.

With regard to yourself, I congratulate you on your change of scene & work, & on the honours that your learning has won for you.[1] The prospect of reading for examining others would be a pleasant one to me: at least if it involved re-reading books that I once read with the other motive of being examined: for nothing seems more to refurnish the mind than reading old books again: I have no pupils now, having been transferred to Warkworth: & I mifs them. It is good to be compelled to read the great books.

Thank you very much for your reference to your Friend Mr. Forbes: & for the trouble you have had about my historical enquiry. I shall avail myself of his help, when I come to look over my new volume: which is growing to completion. The doings of the Reformation in Ireland were abominable. I am about to fill up a gap that I left open in my Irish part, by putting in Bale's adventures in Ofsory.

I now send you a pamphlet of poems[2] which I have printed at Oxford, at Mr. Daniel's press, where Bridges printed Prometheus. You do not like printing of this limited sort, I know: but apart from that, I shall be glad to know what you think. The London public have given up reading poetry. In fact this is not a literary age: & there seems to be a sort of feeling to retire on Oxford & strive to win the young. You have seen some of the pieces.

---

[1] His appointment to the Chair of Greek in the Royal University, Dublin.
[2] Odes and Eclogues / by / Richard Watson Dixon / Printed / at Oxford by Henry Daniel / 1884. 100 copies. Price 5 shillings.

I think you must have some poems of your own that I have not seen, & should be very glad to see, if you could let me conveniently. Bridges perhaps has some. I will ask him, when I write.

I have received this morning from Coventry Patmore a copy of his son's Poems, printed also by Daniel.[1] They seem truly exquisite. Probably you know them. I have to thank you for them really.

I feel that this is a poor answer to your long and kind letter: and I do feel all the force & value of your criticism, being especially pleased that you think Mano's chief quality 'humanity', a new critical term, I think: & a most happy one. Of this I have told Bridges, who agrees. Also I am delighted that you like the 'characterisation': above all Mano himself. Lang in the Saturday[2] said his outline was not clear.

I have been trying to spell out a few Canons of Poetry: feeling, as every one does, the want of some sort of basis for criticism: something definite in principles, to prevent it from being all guess work. Coleridge, I believe, said this was wanted, years ago. What do you think of this, the first?

For the two highest kinds of poetry, dramatic & heroic, blank verse is the only proper vehicle. And, conversely, blank verse is degraded, when it is used for any other kind of poetry.

Corollary. Inferior kinds of poetry, narrative, pastoral, didactic, 'idyllic', and others employ an improper vehicle when they are written in blank verse. Blank verse has been more freely applied to these inferior kinds in the present age than ever before. In proportion as the two highest kinds have been disused, their proper metrical form has been transferred to others.

I may as well go on—

2. For long poems, that are not of the highest kind, the couplet measure or some stanza are proper.

---

[1] Poems by Henry John Patmore, with a biographical note by Gertrude Patmore. Henry Daniel: Oxford, 1884. 125 copies.

[2] See NOTE J.

3. Long poems ought to be written in one measure only. The practice of breaking long narrative poems with lyrics, brought in by Scott & Byron, & universally continued now, is the gravest innovation.

I have some more in mind: but what do you think of these? May be they are nought: but here is another—

Poems in any stanza are of inferior form to poems in the continuous measure of blank or even couplet verse.

With all affectionate regards I am, My dear Friend,

Yours always

R. W. Dixon

XXXI B

Warkworth Vic. 9 July 1884

My dear Friend,—Do not think because I have been long in writing that I have neglected you in thought. I have been & am distrefsed by the news of your illnefs, or at least prostration of strength: & have had you almost constantly in my mind. I wish it lay in my power to do anything. Will you let me know how you are? I have not yet written to your Friends about the Irish Mifsion, tho I had a very kind reply to my first letter from Mr. Forbes. I have been pushing on to the end of my 3.d vol. & the reign of Edward VI, & have now got to the last few pages; after that I shall write to some of them, certainly to Mr. Forbes.

It is not unlikely that Bridges will come to pay me a visit soon, but he has not fixed the time yet. I wish you could see this place.

Do you know anything of an American poet named Street?[1] He seems good from extracts.

I am glad of your good opinion of Odes & Eclogues.[2]

Ever your affec.te Friend

R. W. Dixon

[1] Presumably Alfred Billings Street (1811–81), author of *The Burning of Schenectady, and other Poems* (1842), *Frontenac, or the Atotarbo of the Iroquois, a Metrical Romance* (1849), and *Forest Pictures in the Adirondacks* (1865).
[2] The letter containing this opinion is missing.

XXXII

Milltown Park, Milltown. Oct. 25 1884.

MY DEAR FRIEND,—I am heartily ashamed of myself that I never answered your most kind and comforting letter received on Galway Bay in the summer. Neither do I answer it now, but only say that I am, thank God, much better since then and now drowned in the last and worst of five examinations. I have 557 papers on hand: let those who have been thro' the like say what that means. At this most inopportune time Mr Tom Arnold has asked me to write a short notice of you for the forthcoming new edition of his handbook of English Literature and somehow or other I must do it. Therefore please fill up the following and send it me without delay here (where I am come for quiet).[1]

Add any particular you like, but I do not say they or even all the above can appear, so short is the space at my disposal.

I am your affectionate friend

GERARD M. HOPKINS S.J.

XXXII A

Warkworth Vic. 27 Oct. 1884

MY DEAR FRIEND,—I am so glad to hear from you again, the news of your better health: of which I had heard from Bridges, but glad to be further confirmed. I write in haste, for I am like you nearly stiffled[2] with[3] work. I shall be all week writing against time: not for gain, for that I seldom do: but at my Bishop's command.

Curiously, I had a letter fr. Bridges by the post of yours, & also from Fr. Forbes: to whom you referred me.

He cannot help me: so I send the paper I sent him, to be filled by you, or some one you may perchance give it to, at y.ʳ

---

[1] A 'rough draft' to be used by R. W. D. follows, but is omitted since the latter supplies the information himself. See p. 124.

[2] Thus in MS.   [3] MS. 'with with'.

leisure, with a few ordinary facts about the Mifsion of yr Society to Ireland. I only want to sketch it: but have no ordinary materials. He mentions Mac Arthy's Collections in Irish Ch. Hist. which I have not. You will see I want to make an ordinary paragraph to complete my Irish part. In utter haste

Your aff fr^d

R. W. Dixon

Me.

Now *Vicar* of W & H. C. of C. born 1833, at Islington: son of Dr. Dixon a celebrated Wesleyan Minister, grandson of R. A. Watson author of the chief text books of the same body:[1] educated at King Edw. Sch. Birmingham, & Pembroke Coll. Ox. friendship of B. Jones, W. Morris, & others with whom he was associated in undertaking the Oxford & Cambridge Magazine, in 1856, of Praeraphaelite principles: engaged on H. of C. of Eng. *on a gt. scale*, of wh. 3 vols have appeared: published in 1859[2] Christs Company, in 1863[3] Historical Odes, in 1883 Mano, in 1884 Odes & Eclogues.

XXXIII

University College, Stephen's Green. Dublin. Nov. 24 1884

My dear friend,—You may be delayed by the want of the information you asked for and I must not keep you longer waiting.[4] Fr. Edmund Hogan, to whom I applied, was then suffering from ulcers of the cornea, a sad blow to a devoted student like him, suddenly and unexpectedly fallen: the evil was in process of cure, but he can scarcely expect the full use of his eyesight again. He answered my enquiries, by word of mouth, much as follows.

(1) John Codur's appointment was cancelled: the document

---

[1] Here 'Leicestershire family' cancelled.   [2] An error for 1861.
[3] 1864 on title-page.
[4] The paper sent by R. W. D. exists, and on it are notes made by G. M. H.; but it is omitted here since this letter contains the information in a fuller form.

cancelling it and appointing Brouet (or Broet) and Salmeron instead/exists.

(2) Brouet and Salmeron went, accompanied by Zapata (not Zapota); Brouet was to take the lead and be the spokesman with persons of consequence. (He was a Picard, remarkable for gentleness of disposition, perhaps of birth. Salmeron was a most able commentator on Scripture, as his remains prove). Zapata was a novice. St. Ignatius has assigned to the noviceship six *experimenta*, tests or ordeals of fitness—hospital-nursing, catechising or preaching, the Long Retreat (or making the full 30 days of the Spiritual Exercises), begging, pilgrimage, and I forget what else. The journey might be treated as involving two or three of these for Zapata. He was a man of position and means, had been Notary Apostolic, and bore the expense of the journey. But afterwards he said that it was unbecoming in a member of the Society to preach from a barrel in the streets, which coming to St. Ignatius' ears he dismissed him as unfit. He remained however on good terms with ours.

(3) They were forced to go by Scotland. James received them well and forwarded them, but it was thought that the information of them which reached Henry came from him or his court.

(4) They were 42 days only in Ireland. Their mission was not a success: the chiefs or nobles were then in much the condition of the English nobility, trimming to the king.

(5) 'Unlettered [I presume not absolutely ignorant but unlearned] clergy.' Fr. Hogan thinks the bulk of the clergy were unlearned, the Tridentine reforms not having been carried out, but that there were some learned men.

Most of the above is to be found in Orlandini's 'semi-official' or even Crétineau-Joly's semi-officious Histories of the S. J. and in lives of St. Ignatius: I knew a good deal of it myself. Further information as to places and persons visited may be had, if you care for it, in Fr. Hogan's *Hibernia Ignatiana* (privately printed, but I cd. procure and lend you a copy) and in certain numbers of the *Irish Ecclesiastical Record*, which I could consult for you.

He further added this. In 1559 Fr. Wolfe S.J. came to Ireland with the powers but not the name of Apostolic Nuntius, and since that time there have always been Jesuits in Ireland.* There was a working Province, with perhaps 15 houses, e.g. 3 at Kilkenny, by 1629, at which time they set up a University in Dublin and it flourished till Cromwell.

Let me know whether you will want the further researches I have mentioned. Fr. Hogan promised to look for some loose sheets he thought he had of his book containing the part wanted, but since his return to Limerick I have heard no more of it.

The notice of you is to appear in Mr. Arnold's book,[1] but with omissions, made necessary by want of room, of some of my references; for which I am sorry, for I had calculated them, as far as from memory I could, so as to whet the reader's appetite and send him to the spring for more.†

I am your affectionate friend

GERARD M. HOPKINS S.J.

Nov. 27 1884.

* To the suppression 1771.
† For extracts there was not room.

You know that *Prometheus* is now published.[2]

XXXIII A

Warkworth Vicarage, Northumberland. 1 Dec. 1884

MY DEAR FRIEND,—I have just received your Letter: how welcome it is I cannot say, nor how much I thank you for the information you give, tho still more for writing to me so kindly. I had heard the day before from Bridges, asking me to send you his poem of Eros and Psyche:[3] & wrote you a note to accompany it; but was too late for the post, so now need not send it. I was

---

[1] For this tribute, by G. M. H., see NOTE K.
[2] i.e. for general circulation, by Geo. Bell & Sons, 1884.
[3] Published in 1885.

afraid I had troubled you unduly with my inquiries: and am not sure now that I have not: I mean whether I might not have made out for myself enough from accessible sources. But I was ignorant what sources there were. I shall now go to work on what you have sent: and if I want to know more I will ask again: and perhaps ask the loan of Fr. Hogan's work: that is if I were allowed to make reference to it as my authority for anything I might say. Otherwise it would not be useful to me.

All that you tell me of the first Mission, of 1540, is highly interesting: but besides that I want to cover the whole period from 1540 to 1553 (death of Edward VI). Your Society must have returned within that period: because in 1553, or a little earlier, Browne, the Henrician Archb. of Dublin, preached a sermon against them, complaining of their activity and succeſs.

Fr. Hogan, in your letter, seems to imply that they did not return till 1559, when Fr. Wolfe came.

If there were no Jesuits in Ireland between 1540 and 1559, Browne was unveracious: which I can readily suppose from his character.

Please thank Mr. Hogan for his kindneſs whenever you write to him.

I shall be interested to see Mr. Arnold's book: of which I shall hear probably whenever it comes out. It is a thing that I feel much that you have written about me. Perhaps some time you will kindly tell me the title of the work, and how to be had: or where to look for it.

You will find Eros & Psyche a beautiful poem. I have made a few notes on it & sent them to Bridges, at his request: I mean I made them at his request. Prometheus, as you say, is out, & will succeed. There was a very good review in the Academy.[1] Have you seen his Nero? It seemed very good when I read it: especially the metre. He is writing a great deal just now.

You do not say anything about yourself. Bridges told me you were through all that examination work, and ready to

---

[1] The issue of 22 Nov. 1884. See NOTE L.

read anything. I hope the illnefs and prostration, of which you spoke before, is really passed.

I am, My dear Friend,
Yours affectionately

R. W. DIXON

Kindly let me know by a P.C of Psyche's safety.

XXXIII B

Warkworth Vicarage. 19 Jan. 1885

MY DEAR FRIEND,—Will you excuse a hasty note to ask you either to send me the Hibernia Ignatiana, or tell me out of it the places to which the first Irish Mission went, and any incidents related: with permission to refer to the book, and reference given.

The published books to which you referred me are defective in that, they say nothing of the localities.

I have been to London for four days, & rather hoped to have seen Bridges, but he decided not to come up. My 3^{d} volume of Ch. hist. is finished since last July, but still there are many holes to stop, such as this that I write about now.

Your affec^{te} Friend

R. W. DIXON

XXXIII C

Warkworth North^{d}. 19 Mar. 1885.

MY DEAR FRIEND,—I cannot say how much I thank you, or how valuable your help, or how I feel your goodnefs in bestowing so much labour. I have completed my account of the Mifsion: & the footnote with wh. it begins runs thus.

'The following account of the first Jesuit mission into Ireland is compiled from the valuable volume entitled Ibernia Ign. printed by the Soc. Typogr. Dublin. The author is the Reverend Edmond Hogan S.J. who has drawn from materials that seem unknown to the historians of the Order that are generally read.

For my knowledge of this & for other information I am indebted
to my friend the Reverend Gerard Hopkins S.J.'[1]
I have not read all Nero in print yet. It is magnificent

Yours aff. & gratefully

R. W. Dixon

[No further letter for 1885 has been found (though one written in
December by R. W. D. is referred to later by G. M. H.), but the
sonnet that follows, written out by G. M. H., is on a piece of paper,
alone. Concerning it see R. B.'s note (*Poems*, 38): he takes it 'as
apparently later than A, but with errors of copy'. So in l. 7 he
indicates on the MS. where *a* is to be inserted, and writes *swarm* for
throng, and in l. 9 underlines *needs* (which he retains), a word not
found in the other MSS. To judge from the hand-writing it seems
probable that the copy was made near the date it carries.]

TO WHAT SERVES MORTAL BEAUTY?

(sonnet: alexandrines: the mark ⌐¬ over two neighbouring
syllables means that, though one has and the other has not the
metrical stress, in the recitation-stress they are to be about
equal)

To what serves mortal beauty— | dăngerous; does set danc-
Ing blood—the O-seal-that-so | feature, flung prouder form
Than Purcell tune lets tread to? | see : it does this: keeps warm
Men's wits to the things that are; | what good means—where
 a glance
Master more may than gaze, | gaze out of countenance.
Those lovely lads once, wetfresh | windfalls of war's storm,
How then should Gregory, father, | have gleanèd else from
 throng-
Èd Rome? But God to a nation | dealt that day's dear chance.
To man, that needs would worship | block or barren stone,

---

[1] *The History of the Church of England* . . ., vol. iii, footnote pp. 418–19,
where, in the last sentence, 'gifted' is inserted before 'friend', an epithet
which G. M. H. regarded wryly. See vol. i, p. 223.

Our law says Love what are | love's worthiest, were all known;

World's loveliest—men's selves. Self | flashes off frame and face.

What do then? how meet beauty? | Merely meet it; own,

Home at heart, heaven's sweet gift; | then leave, let that alone.
Yea, wish that though, wish all, | God's better beauty, grace.

Aug. 23 1885

XXXIII D

Warkworth Vicarage, Acklington. 21 June 1886

MY DEAR FRIEND,—I am employed by Messrs Routledge the
Publishers to edit a Bible Birthday Book: a collection of texts
& verses of poetry.[1] I want to include at least one of yours.
Bridges gave me the following out of his MS of your poems.

> The dappled die-away
> Cheek, & wimpled lip,
> The gold-wisp, the aery-grey
> Eye, all in fellowship—
> This, all this, beauty blooming,
> This, all this, freshnefs fuming,
> Give God, while worth consuming.[2]

May I take it? if so can you put a text before it?

I have been down at Yattendon with Mrs. Dixon, & greatly
enjoyed my visit. We talked of you several times. I am inserting several pieces from Bridges.[3] What a fine thing his classic
Comedy is.[4]

---

[1] Published in 1887. Routledge published *Mano* and vols. 2 and 3 of his
History; R.W.D.'s second wife was Matilda, eldest daughter of this George
Routledge.

[2] Printed, with minor changes, under 25 May, with the text: As for the
oblation of the first-fruits, ye shall offer them unto the Lord. Leviticus ii. 12.

[3] There are six extracts from R. B.'s poetry (13 Jan., 27 Mar., 11 May,
26 Aug., 7 Sept., 8 Oct.), and one from Coventry Patmore (13 Feb.).

[4] The second draft of *The Feast of Bacchus* was finished on 5 August 1886;
R. W. D. therefore probably saw this play in its first draft on his visit to
Yattendon.

I feel as if I ought to write you a long letter, & would fain do so: but have little to say that you would care to hear. I have been in London a few days, & saw the Colonial Exhibition without caring for it, and the pictures of the year without caring for them. Burne Jones seemed to me still to stand topmost: but I am out of sympathy with him. His great work the Depths of the Sea is very fine, & stood forth as the only serious thing in the Academy.[1] But beyond feeling that, the sort of passionate grandeur, & the powerful drawing, I did not feel that it carried weight or delight. All the other ambitious pictures seemed unendurably bad to me.

I was truly glad & happy to hear from Bridges of the restoration of your health, and of the affection with which all there regarded you.

I shall be bringing out some time this year a small Daniel of lyrics.[2] You know most of them. Will you accept the dedication of them?

Have you ever seen Whistler's works? I saw his little gallery in Bond St. He is a man of great genius, but eccentric. He puzzles me. Ruskin was wrong about him, & did him great injustice. Ruskin is publishing a sort of penitential edition of Modern Painters. He should take the opportunity of repenting about Whistler.

Ever, my dear Friend,
Your affec. friend

R. W. Dixon

Can you send me anything else for the Birthday Book?

[1] Burne-Jones was chosen A.R.A. in 1885, but this was the only picture he exhibited at Burlington House. D.N.B. says: 'Like all who saw it there, the artist found that the picture looked strange and ineffective among its incongruous surroundings.'

[2] Lyrical Poems / By / Richard Watson Dixon / Printed by H. Daniel, Fellow of / Worcester College: Oxford / 1887. 105 copies printed.

XXXIV

University College, St. Stephen's Green, Dublin. June 30 '86

MY DEAR FRIEND,—I am in the midst of my heaviest work of the year, the summer examinations, and not at all fit for them. This is why I delay writing and is some excuse for not earlier answering your former letter; which was however a fault.

There are first two points of what we may call business. The dedication: this is a great honour, which on the one hand I do not like to decline but which nevertheless I have some dread of, for I do not want my name to be before the public. It is true your poems do not command a large public, unhappily; but then the small one might contain enemies, so to call people, of mine. So do which you think best: if you dedicate I am flattered, if you do not I am reassured.[1]

I think there could be no objection to my lines appearing in the Birthday Book, especially anonymously (as I should wish),[2] but I ought to get a formal leave and will. However I should tell you that the poem in question is in three stanzas: did you know that?[3] Nevertheless the first, the one you quote, might stand by itself. If so the text should be something about First-fruits: there must be several that would do, but I think of none just now. The second line had better be 'Cheek and the wimpled lip'[4] and the count made up to six. And the stopping 'This, all this, beauty' etc is cumbrous: it is better 'This, all this beauty'.[5] I have nothing else to send, but something new might strike me. There is a 3-stanza piece made at a wedding that possibly might do,[6] but I rather think not: it is too personal and, I believe, too plainspoken.

I saw the Academy. There was one thing, not a picture, which I much preferred to everything else there—Hamo Thornycroft's statue of the *Sower*, a truly noble work and to me a new light.

---

[1] The book is 'Dedicated to the Reverend Gerard Hopkins by the Author'.

[2] The stanza has *Hopkins* at the foot.   [3] *Poems*, 24.

[4] This change was not made.   [5] This change was made.

[6] *Poems*, 28.

saw the Academy. There was one thing; a picture which I much preferred to everything else there — name thornycroft's statue of
62
... a truly noble work and to me a new light. It was like Frederick walker's pictures put into stone and indeed was no doubt partly due to his influence. The genius of that man, how Walker, was amazing; he was cut off by death like Keats and his promise and performance were in painting as brilliant as Keats's in poetry; in fact hardly a man with purer genius for painting ever lived. The sense of beauty lay so exquisite; it cmy to other painters? work as poetry of O Prose; his loss was irretrievable.

It was like Frederick Walker's pictures put into stone and indeed was no doubt partly due to his influence. The genius of that man, poor Walker, was amazing: he was cut off by death like Keats and his promise and performance were in painting as brilliant as Keats's in poetry; in fact I doubt if a man with purer genius for painting ever lived. The sense of beauty was so exquisite; it was to other painters' work as poetry is to prose: his loss was irretrievable.[1] Now no one admires more keenly than I do the gifts that go into Burne Jones's works, the fine genius, the spirituality, the invention; but they leave me deeply dissatisfied as well, where Walker's works more than satisfy. It is their technical imperfection I can not get over, the bad, the unmasterly drawing—as it appears to me to be. They are not masterly. Now this is the artist's most essential quality, masterly execution: it is a kind of male gift and especially marks off men from women, the begetting one's thought on paper, on verse, on whatever the matter is; the life must be conveyed into the work and be displayed there, not suggested as having been in the artist's mind: otherwise the product is one of those hen's-eggs that are good to eat and look just like live ones but never hatch (I think they are called wind eggs: I believe most eggs for breakfast *are* wind eggs and none the worse for it).—Now it is too bad of me to have compared Burne Jones's beautiful and original works to wind-eggs; moreover on better consideration it strikes me that the mastery I speak of is not so much the male quality in the mind as a puberty in the life of that quality. The male quality is the creative gift, which he markedly has. But plainly, while artists may differ indefinitely in the degree and kind or variety of their natural gifts, all shd., as artists, have come, at all events shd. in time come, to the puberty, the manhood of those gifts: that should be common to all, above it the gifts may differ.

[1] Frederick Walker (1840–75) was mainly self-trained, and known as an illustrator before he exhibited his first oil picture at the Academy in 1863. 'He affords perhaps the most conspicuous modern instance of an artist reaching beauty and unity through an almost blind obedience to his own instincts and emotions' (*D.N.B.*). See his *Life and Letters*, by J. G. Marks.

It may be remarked that some men exercise a deep influence on their own age in virtue of certain powers at that time original, new, and stimulating, which afterwards ceasing to stimulate their fame declines; because it was not supported by an execution, an achievement equal to the power. For nothing but fine execution survives long. This was something of Rossetti's case perhaps.

There is a Scotch painter Macbeth whom I much admire.[1] My brother Arthur, who is a painter too, took me to Macbeth's studio when I was last in town. There happened to be little of Macbeth's own there then, but he was employed on an etching of Walker's *Fisherman's Shop* for Messrs. Agnew and the original was of course with him. It is not a work that I care for very much except so far as I revere everything that Walker did (I remember the news of his death gave me a shock as if it had been a near friend's), though artists greatly admire the technic of it; but there were other etchings by Macbeth and other reproductions of Walker's pieces and most of them new to me, the *Ferry* I think it is called (an upper-Thames riverside scene), the *Plough* (a divine work),[2] the *Mushroom Gatherers*,[3] and others. If you have not yet studied Walker's work you have a new world of beauty to open and go in. You shd. also study where you can *North's*[4] things. It was my brother drew my attention to him. It seems Walker—I do not know that he studied under North but he learnt methods from him: 'North' said someone in vulgar phrase to my brother 'learnt', that is taught, 'Walker to paint'. He survived his pupil, if Walker was that. His land-

[1] R. W. Macbeth, A.R.A., etcher of many of Walker's pictures.

[2] Exhibited at the Academy in 1870; a work that has poetry, movement, passion, strength, and a strange 'newness'. The artist evidently shared G. M. H.'s admiration for virility and native grace (e.g. *Harry Ploughman, Poems*, 43). See Marks, op. cit., pp. 193–4 for Walker's description, in a letter, of what he intended to do in this picture.

[3] Unfinished: the artist was working on it towards the end of his life.

[4] J. W. North, A.R.A., who was with Walker at Whymper's (the wood engraver) and remained his friend and one of his chief correspondents. He has left several descriptions of Walker. See Marks, op. cit.

scapes are of a beautiful and poetical delicacy and truth at once. But I have seen very little of his.

I agree to Whistler's striking genius—feeling for what I call *inscape* (the very soul of art); but then his execution is so negligent, unpardonably so sometimes (that was, I suppose, what Ruskin particularly meant by 'throwing the pot of paint in the face of the public'): *his* genius certainly has not come to puberty.

Now something on music. A piece of mine, called, not by my wish, a madrigal in the programme, is to be performed at a school-concert in Dublin tomorrow. It is *Who is Sylvia?* set as a duet and chorus, the tune made very long ago, the harmonies lately set (and very great fears about their puberty entertained). I made it for a string orchestra. And I am very slowly but very elaborately working at 'Does the South Wind' for solos, chorus, and strings. Some years ago I went from Glasgow, where I was, one day to Loch Lomond and landed at Inversnaid (famous through Wordsworth and Matthew Arnold) for some hours. There I had an inspiration of a tune. The disproportion is wonderful between the momentary conception of an air and the long long gestation of its setting. I endeavour to make the under parts each a flowing and independent melody and they cannot be independently invented, they must be felt for along a few certain necessary lines enforced by the harmony. It is astonishing to see them come; but in reality they are in nature bound up (besides many others) with the tune of the principal part and there is, I am persuaded, a world of profound mathematics in this matter of music: indeed no one could doubt that.

I have written a few sonnets: that is all I have done in poetry for some years.

I have not seen Bridges' comedy.

Swinburne has written for the *Times* an ode on the crisis,[1] Somebody called it a rigmarole and I cd. not say it was not: on the contrary everything he writes is rigmarole. But I wonder

---

[1] *The Commonweal, a Song for Unionists*, printed in the issue of 1 July 1886, and published in *A Channel Passage and other Poems*. It contains bitter lines on Gladstone.

how he finds it suits him to be clerical, as this ode with appeals
to conscience and declaiming against assassination is. Moreover
there was an earlier ode of his in honour of the 'Manchester
Martyrs',[1] as the Irish call them: so then he has changed as
much as Gladstone. As they neither of them have any principles
it is no wonder. But the passage about Gordon and so on is to
the point.[2] It seems to me that 'bad is the best' that can happen
now. With this sad thought I must conclude and am your
affectionate friend

GERARD M. HOPKINS S.J.

Some hindrance happened and the madrigal was not sung.
If it had been I could not have heard it, for I was helping to
save and damn the studious youth of Ireland.

July 3 1886.

You speak of 'powerful drawing' in Burne Jones's picture.
I recognise it in the mermaid's face and in the treatment of her
fishments and fishmanship, the tailfin turning short and flat-
tening to save striking the ground—a stroke of truly artistic
genius; but the drowned youth's knees and feet are very crude
and unsatisfactory in drawing, as it seemed to me.

[3]I have found your former letter, as old as December last,[4]
and must add a little more.

The sonnet of Gray's that you ask about is the wellknown
one (the only one, I daresay) 'In vain to me': I remarked on its
rhythmical beauty, due partly to the accent being rather
trochaic than iambic. Wordsworth says somewhere of it that

---

[1] 'An Appeal to England' [for the condemned Fenian prisoners], 20 Nov.
1867: included in *Songs before Sunrise*, 1870.
[2] 'Far and near the world bears witness of our wisdom, courage, honour;
    Egypt knows if there our fame burns bright or dim.
Let but England trust as Gordon trusted, soon shall come upon her
    Such deliverance as our daring brought on him.'
[3] What follows is marked by R. B., 'Undated fragment', and was placed
here by him. Whether it formed part of this letter or another is not certain.
The visit mentioned at the end was presumably made on 6 May 1886 (see
vol. i, CXXXII).
[4] This letter is missing.

it is 'evident' the only valuable part of it is (I believe) 'For other notes' and the quatrain that follows.[1] Such a criticism is rude at best, since in a work of art having so strong a unity as a sonnet one part which singly is less beautiful than another part may be as necessary to the whole effect, like the plain shaft in a column and so on. But besides what he calls evident is not so, nor true.

You make a criticism on Handel. I have the very same feeling about him and you 'tell me my own dream', that 'one can never hear five bars of him without feeling that something great is beginning, something full of life'. A piece of his at a concert seems to flutter the dovecot of the rest of them, to be a hawk among poultry. The immediateness of the impression must be due, I suppose, to his power being conveyed into smaller sections of his work than other men's and not needing accumulation for its effect.

I was glad of an appreciative review of your third volume in the *Academy* (I think) and much interested.[2] Would I could read the work! but I cannot under present, which are permanent, circumstances do that.

I could wish you had been elected to that Chair.[3] But 'life is a short blanket'—profoundest of homely sayings: great gifts and great opportunities are more than life spares to one man. It is much if we get something, a spell, an innings at all. See how the great conquerors were cut short, Alexander, Caesar just seen. Above all Christ our Lord: his career was cut short and, whereas he would have wished to succeed by success—for it is insane to lay yourself out for failure, prudence is the first of the cardinal virtues, and he was the most prudent of men—

[1] Preface to the Second Edition (1800) of *Lyrical Ballads*. This is not an accurate statement of Wordsworth's criticism: he excepts five lines—6–8, 13–14.

[2] In the issue of 27 Feb. 1886: a very complimentary review in four columns by Mandell Creighton, which begins with a long paragraph praising the style and temper of the work.

[3] In 1885 R. W. D. stood for the professorship of Poetry at Oxford, but withdrew his candidature before the election.

nevertheless he was doomed to succeed by failure; his plans were baffled, his hopes dashed, and his work was done by being broken off undone. However much he understood all this he found it an intolerable grief to submit to it. He left the example: it is very strengthening, but except in that sense it is not consoling.

I passed a delightful day at Yattendon. Mrs. Bridges not as I had fancied her (which was but faintly), but none the worse for that.

XXXIV A

Warkworth. 28 July 1886

MY DEAR, DEAR FRIEND,—I cannot now answer your precious Letter: but must thank you for it.

I have inserted your 'first fruits' piece, & propose, if you do not forbid, to put your name to it thus, G. (or else Gerard) Hopkins S.J.[1]

I have heard from Bridges to-day.

I dedicate to you my Lyrical Poems: but have not heard of them since I sent them to Daniel months ago. His health prevents, I fear, the immediate publication.

Your aff. friend

R. W. DIXON

XXXV

University College, Stephen's Green, Dublin. Aug. 7 '86.

MY DEAR FRIEND,—The note you speak of did not reach me and no doubt was never posted, for the post never misses (if there is a never in human things) and every alternative should be exhausted before we come to that. (And therefore I say that the number of the *Academy* which shd. have come to hand this morning was also not posted or, what is more likely, has gone astray in the house.)

If the poem is printed it may rest, but I am going to see the Provincial tomorrow or next day and will ask him about it. I ought to have settled this before; but since I last wrote I have

[1] See p. 132, note 2.

been altogether overwhelmed with examination-work, six or seven weeks of it without any break, Sundays and weekdays. Even now—but it is no use talking of it.

Mr. Rawnsley's name is quite unknown to me.[1]

It is not possible for me to do anything, unless a sonnet, and that rarely, in poetry with a fagged mind and a continual anxiety; but there are things at which I can, so far as time serves, work, if it were only by snatches. For instance I am writing (but I am almost sure I never shall have written) a sort of popular account of Light and the Ether. Popular is not quite the word; it is not meant to be easy reading, for such a difficult subject can only be made easy by a very summary and sketchy treatment; rather it is meant for the lay or unprofessional student who will read carefully so long as there are no mathematics and all technicalities are explained; and my hope is to explain things thoroughly and make the matter to such a reader, as far as I go in it, perfectly intelligible. No such account exists and scientific books, especially in English, are very unsatisfactory. The study of physical science has, unless corrected in some way, an effect the very opposite of what one would suppose. One would think it might materialise people (no doubt it does make them or, rather I shd. say, they become materialists; but that is not the same thing: they do not believe in Matter more but in God less); but in fact they seem to end in conceiving only of a world of formulas, with its being properly speaking in thought, towards which the outer world acts as a sort of feeder, supplying examples for literary purposes. And they go so far as to think the rest of mankind are in the same state of mind as themselves. I daresay I may gather together some illustrations of this: one will serve now. 'It is very remarkable' says Tait[2] on *Light* 'how slowly the human race has reached some even of the simplest, facts of optics [he rather means laws]. We can easily understand how constant experience must have forced on men the

---

[1] The Rev. Hardwicke Drummond Rawnsley (1851–1920), whose name and work are intimately associated with the Lake District.

[2] *Light*, by Peter Guthrie Tait, 1884.

conviction [as if they were resisting it: the force would have been to make them think the contrary] that light usually moves in straight lines—i.e. that we see an object in the direction in which it really lies. [Where else shd. one expect to see it?] But' etc.

It will in any case be a pity for S.J. to have been added to my name in the book, for the letters act like italics, asterisks, or rubric.

Some learned lady having shewn by the flora that the season of the action in *Hamlet* is from March to May, a difficulty is raised about the glowworm's ineffectual fire in the first act, since glowworms glow chiefly from May to September. Mr. Furnival having consulted an authority learns that the grub, though not so easily found, shines nearly as bright as the fullgrown worm, that is beetle, and begins in March, and so all is saved. Does not this strike you as great trifling? Shakspere had the finest faculty of observation of all men that ever breathed, but it is ordinary untechnical observation, neither scientific nor even, like a farmer's professional, and he might overlook that point of season. But if he knew it he would likely enough neglect it. There are some errors you must not make, as an eclipse at the halfmoon or a lobster 'the Cardinal of the seas',[1] but others do not matter and convention varies with regard to them. If I am not mistaken, there are notorious and insoluble inconsistencies in *Hamlet*, due to Shakspere's having recast the play expressly for Burbage, who was elderly, 'short, stout, and scant of breath' (or something of the sort), without taking the trouble to correct throughout accordingly—not even wishing I dare say; for no one can so conceive of Hamlet's person. Besides there are inconsistencies in the Iliad, Aeneid, Don Quixote, Three Musketeers, and so on; it is a frailty of literature. And indeed on reflection the defence makes the matter worse. For few of the audience could know that glowworms do shine, if you look well for them, in March. So that Shakspere would have

---

[1] Perhaps the origin of this phrase is to be found in Rabelais, *Œuvres* (Champion, 1913), t. ii, *Gargantua*, chap. xxxix, ll. 50–2.

been breaking Aristotle's rule, that in art likely seeming fiction
is better than unlikely seeming fact.

By the by, why should Wordsworth-worship be 'a difficult
thing'? It is a common one now, is it not? Not *the* common,
but like soldiers in a crowd, not a numerous but a notable fact.
Did you see what Lord Selborne[1] lately said? What I suppose
grows on people is that Wordsworth's particular grace, his
charisma, as theologians say, has been granted in equal measure
to so very few men since times was—to Plato and who else?
I mean his spiritual insight into nature; and this they perhaps
think is above all the poet's gift? It is true, if we sort things,
so that art is art and philosophy philosophy, it seems rather the
philosopher's than the poet's: at any rate he had it in a sovereign
degree. He had a 'divine philosophy' and a lovely gift of verse;
but in his work there is nevertheless *beaucoup à redire*: it is due
to the universal fault of our literature, its weakness is rhetoric.
The strictly poetical insight and inspiration of our poetry seems
to me to be of the very finest, finer perhaps than the Greek;
but its rhetoric is inadequate—seldom firstrate, mostly only just
sufficient, sometimes even below par. By rhetoric I mean all
the common and teachable element in literature, what gram-
mar is to speech, what thoroughbass is to music, what theatrical
experience gives to playwrights. If you leave out the embroidery
(to be sure the principal thing) of for instance the *Excursion*
and look only at the groundwork and stuff of the web is it not
fairly true to say 'This will never do'? There does seem to be
a great deal of dulness, superfluity, aimlessness, poverty of plan.
I remember noticing as a boy, it was the discovery of a trade
secret, how our poets treat *spirit* and its compounds as one syllable:
it is, though founded really on a mistake, the mere change of
pronunciation, a beautiful tradition of the poets. Wordsworth
had told himself or been told this trifle: why did he not learn
or someone tell him that sonnets have a natural *charpente* and

[1] Lord Selborne delivered the Presidential Address at the final meeting
of the Wordsworth Society on 9 July 1886: for this, see *Wordsworthiana*, ed.
W. Knight, 1889, pp. 277-88.

structure never, or at least seldom, to be broken through? For want of knowing this his inspired sonnets, εὔμορφοι κολοσσοί,[1] suffer from 'hernia', and combine the tiro's blunder with the master's perfection.

Believe me your affectionate friend

GERARD HOPKINS. Aug. 9.

XXXV A

Warkworth Vic. Northumberland. 25 Sept. 1886

MY DEAR FRIEND,—Would you mind looking over the enclosed,[2] & making any suggestion or objection or correction.

I am in no hurry for a week or so. You will perhaps not have the time or inclination. If so do not, please, force yourself. I am sorry to leave no time to write, but will soon, I hope, more fully.

Your affc friend

R. W. DIXON

XXXVI

11 Church Street, Tremadoc, North Wales. Sept. 30 1886.

MY DEAR FRIEND,—Your enclosure very opportunely reached me this morning in this remote and beautiful spot, where I am bringing a pleasant holiday to an end. My companion and colleague left me last night, being called to Dublin on University business more pressing than mine. The weather is quite broken and the soldier in Mrs. Evans's weatherclock stands out of his box with a dismal effrontery, while the maiden sulks, like Weeping Winefred, indoors.

My situation is that Wild Wales breathes poetry on the one hand and that my landlady gives me the heartiest breakfasts on the other; it is indigenous to this part of the country, for

[1] 'Beautiful statues.' Aeschylus, *Agamemnon*, 416.

[2] The proofs of *Ulysses and Calypso*, afterwards the first of *Lyrical Poems*, 1887.

the Rev. P. B. Williams A.B. Rector of Llanrug and Llanberis in his *Tourist's Guide through the County of Caernarvon* ibid. 1821 says of Snowdon 'It was then that the thought of the great Creator . . . at whose nod they shall crumble into dust!

> These are thy glorious works,
>   Parent of good . . .
>   . . . how wondrous then!

Parties generally take cold meat with them, and a bottle either of Wine, or Spirits, and dine' etc, p. 122.

I have read your beautiful poem and will shortly return you the proofs with such slight comments as may occur. At present I have a difficulty about 'Whence in her secret cave'. Parallels I daresay may be found and, if not, the expression may be innovated; but in itself it appears incorrect, for *whence* would seem to mean only *from which place*, but you mean *from a place at which*.

In the meantime guided by the Rector of Llanrug and Llanberis I am thinking of taking a hard-boiled egg with me and rhapsodising either the Vale of Ffestiniog or for a second time Pont Aberglaslyn, which not to have seen, as till a few days ago I never had, is a dreadful underbred ignorance.

I am your affectionate friend

GERARD M. HOPKINS.

I have long wished to write a tragedy of St. Winefred and had some fragments of it done, and since I have been here I have got on with it a little, with promise of more. It is in an alexandrine verse, which I sometimes expand to 7 or 8 feet, very hard to manage but very effective when well used: I think I mentioned this point before.

I have a few odd sonnets accumulated over some time which I must try and let you have.

I have the *Castle of Otranto* here and incline to think it is great rubbish. In one place a hollow groan is heard, which both Theodore and Matilda conclude 'to be the effect of pent-up vapours'.

XXXVI A

Warkworth. 18 Oct. 1886.

My DEAR FRIEND,—I am greatly obliged by your kindnefs in criticising Ulysses & Calypso in the midst of so much work of your own. I have benefited much by what you say about it: making several important alterations.

I do not altogether understand your opinions about mythology, of which I have heard through Bridges, who shewed me a letter about it.[1] I think the Greek mythology very beautiful; most beautiful in the hands of the dramatists, more than in Homer: and probably the dramatists looked on it in somewhat the way that English poets have, as a storehouse. Bridges in his Prometheus treats it finely: indicating at the same time (I think) that there are heights above it: in the passages about primordial fire, & fate. It has been a source of beauty to all poetry.

You spoke of Wordsworth. I quite agree as to his healing power: which is perhaps the best quality of poetry. In my opinion his finest poem is The Old Cumberland Beggar. He is very great in that function of the seer's healing & consolation. Unfortunately there is so often a sense of baulk, in his lyrics particularly. The image is conveyed, but with a kind of unhappinefs: 'Lord of the vale, astounding flood.'[2] 'Little cyclops with one eye,'[3] of the daisy. 'He was a lovely youth I guefs' &c.[4] In fact nearly all his best known lyrics have that misfortune. This has kept me from being 'a Wordsworthian', in the full sense. On the other hand, in metres that suit him, he is almost sometimes matchlefsly vivid: e.g.

> While a dark storm before my sight
> Was yielding, on the mountain h[e]ight
> Loose vapours have I watched, that won
> Prismatic colours from the sun.[5]

---

[1] See vol. i, pp. 216–17.

[2] *Memorials of a Tour in Scotland, II. Composed at Cora Linn, in sight of Wallace's Tower,* l. 1.

[3] *To the Daisy* (second poem, 1802), l. 25.   [4] *Ruth,* ll. 37 sqq.

[5] *Written in a Blank Leaf of Macpherson's Ossian,* ll. 5–8, with *the* for *a* in l. 6.

And this not for the sake of the picture, but in the midst of a lot of consolation.

I am very much prefsed with work, or I should like to go on talking with you. Thank you very much for your former delightful letter. One thing that has stood in the way of Wordsworth with me is the extravagance of some of the claims made for him. Pattison said the Ode about Immortality was the second poem in the language, Lycidas being the first. It is constantly called the Great Ode. I do not see that it is particularly good (for Wordsworth, or as Wordsworth), much lefs great. But Wordsworth was a great poet.

Thank you again for the valuable services you have done to U. & C.

I wish you would send me some of your own: you spoke of some sonnets &c.

Your affec^{te} friend

R. W. DIXON

The short piece (perhaps a sonnet?) called 'Sky prospect' is worth any number of Great Odes.[1] It is as good as a tour to read his memorials of Tours: how fine are the lines on Trajan's Column. e.g.[2]

XXXVII

University College, St. Stephen's Green, Dublin. Oct. 23 1886

MY DEAR FRIEND,—There are some points in your letter I have to reply to. First of the Greek mythology. Of course I agree with the rest of the world in admiring its beauty. Above everything else the Greeks excelled in art: now their mythology was the earliest of their arts that have in any way survived, older in the main than Homer's poems, and is I daresay as much more beautiful than other mythologies as Homer's epic is than other epics; speaking of epic proper. It is free from that cumber of

---

[1] *Sky-Prospect—From the Plain of France* (xxxiii of *Memorials of a Tour on the Continent*, 1820).
[2] *The Pillar of Trajan* (1826).

meaningless and childish rubbish which interrupts and annoys one even in the midst of fine invention in for instance the Irish legends.

This however is to speak of it as stories, as fairytales, well invented well told fairytales. But mythology is something else besides fairytale: it is religion, the historical part of religion. It must have been this side of the Greek mythology I was speaking of in that letter; and could I speak too severely of it? First it is as history untrue. What is untrue history? Nothing and worse than nothing. And that history religion? Still worse. I cannot enter on this consideration without being brought face to face with the great fact of heathenism. Now we mostly pass heathenism by as a thing utterly departed, which indeed it is not but in India rank and flourishing; but if for once we face it what are we to say of it? For myself literally words would fail me to express the loathing and horror with which I think of it and of man setting up the work of his own hands, of that hand within the mind the imagination, for God Almighty who made heaven and earth. Still he might set up beings perfect in their kind. But the Greek gods are rakes, and unnatural rakes. Put that aside too; put yourself in the position of a man who like Homer first believes in them, next forgets or passes over their wickedness: even so are the Greek gods majestic, awe inspiring, as Homer that great Greek genius represents them? They are not. The Indian gods are imposing, the Greek are not. Indeed they are not brave, not self controlled, they have no manners, they are not gentlemen and ladies. They clout one another's ears and blubber and bellow. You will say this is Homer's fun, like the miracle-plays of Christendom. Then where is his earnest about them? At their best they remind me of some company of beaux and fashionable world at Bath in its palmy days or Tunbridge Wells or what not. Zeus is like the Major in *Pendennis* handsomer and better preserved sitting on Olympus as behind a club-window and watching Danae and other pretty seamstresses cross the street—not to go farther. You will think this is very Philistine and vulgar and be pained. But I am pained: this is the light in which the matter strikes me, the only one in which it will; and I do think it is the true light.

But I grant that the Greek mythology is very susceptible of fine treatment, allegorical treatment for instance, and so treated gives rise to the most beautiful results. No wonder: the moral evil is got rid of and the pure art, morally neutral and artistically so rich, remains and can be even turned to moral uses.

The letter you saw must have been in criticism of Bridges' *Ulysses*. I was set against that play by the appearance of Athene in the prologue or opening. Bridges took her almost seriously: so then did I, and was disgusted. But I hold it was a false step of his: the heathen gods cannot be taken seriously on our stage; nowadays they cannot even be taken humorously; and it would tell against the play's success. I know that was a noble play; but I had another objection besides to it, the great severity, the aridity even and joylessness of the lyrics. So I damped and damned and must have hurt Bridges.

I feel now I am warm and my hand is in for my greater task, Wordsworth's ode; and here, my dear friend, I must earnestly remonstrate with you; must have it out with you. Is it possible that—but it is in black and white: you say the ode is not, for Wordsworth, good; and much less great.

To say it was the second ode in the language was after all only a comparative remark: one might maintain, though I daresay you will not, that English is not rich in odes. The remark therefore is not of itself extravagant. But if the speaker had said that it was one of the dozen or of the half dozen finest odes of the world I must own that to me there would have seemed no extravagance. There have been in all history a few, a very few men, whom common repute, even where it did not trust them, has treated as having had something happen to them that does not happen to other men, as having *seen something*, whatever that really was. Plato is the most famous of these. Or to put it as it seems to me I must somewhere have written to you or to somebody, human nature in these men saw something, got a shock; wavers in opinion, looking back, whether there was anything in it or no; but is in a tremble ever since. Now what Wordsworthians mean is, what would seem to be the growing mind of the English speaking world and may perhaps come to be that of the world at large/is that in Wordsworth when he wrote that ode human nature got another of those shocks, and the tremble from it is spreading. This opinion I do strongly share; I am, ever since I knew the ode, in that tremble. You know what happened to crazy Blake, himself a most poetically electrical subject both active and passive, at his first hearing: when the reader came to 'The pansy at my feet' he fell into a hysterical excitement. Now commonsense forbid we should take on like these unstrung hysterical creatures: still it was a proof of the power of the shock.

The ode itself seems to me better than anything else I know of Wordsworth's, so much as to equal or outweigh everything else he wrote: to me it appears so. For Wordsworth was an imperfect artist, as you say: as his matter varied in importance and as he varied in insight (for he had a profound insight of some things and little of others) so does the value of his work vary. Now the interest and importance of the matter were here of the highest, his insight was at its very deepest, and hence to my mind the extreme value of the poem.

His powers rose, I hold, with the subject: the execution is so fine. The rhymes are so musically interlaced, the rhythms so happily succeed (surely it is a magical change 'O joy that in our embers'), the diction throughout is so charged and steeped in beauty and yearning (what a stroke 'The moon doth with delight'!). It is not a bit of good my going on if, which is to me so strange in you and disconcerting, you do not feel anything of this. But I do hope you will reconsider it. For my part I shd. think St. George and St. Thomas of Canterbury wore roses in heaven for England's sake on the day that ode, not without their intercession, was penned; for, to better a little the good humoured old cynical proverb, 'When grace of God is gone and spent Then learning is most excellent' and goes to make the greatness of a nation—which is what I urge on Bridges and now on you, to get yourselves known and be up betimes on our Parnassus.

Now no more. I will copy you soon some odd ends, sonnets. Have you my song for my play of *St. Winefred* called *The Leaden Echo and the Golden Echo*? If not I will try and copy it as time serves: I never did anything more musical.

May the Muses bring you to a better mind. May God Almighty, and this without reserve. I am your affectionate friend

GERARD M. HOPKINS S.J.

Oct. 24. Examinations over and I begin lecturing tomorrow.

XXXVII A

Warkworth. 25 Oct. 1886.

MY DEAR FRIEND,—I can only write to thank you for your Letter: I go tomorrow to Newcastle to the Diocesan Conference, where I have to read a paper, which now occupies me. I am much touched by your letter, & will certainly give all attention to Wordsworth's Ode. Indeed after what you say I feel certain I must be mistaken about it. Pattison said it was the second poem, not ode, in the language.

This is to acknowledge your letter and thank you for it. It was the letter on Ulysses.

Yes, I read your two Voices at Bridges' once: but I have no copy. They produced in me secretly some slight approach to what you say of Blake

Your affec^te Friend

R. W. DIXON

XXXVIII

University College, St. Stephen's Green, Dublin. Jan. 27 '87

MY DEAR FRIEND,—It is long since I heard from you. You sent me no more of your proofs; of which, if I could be of any use, I am sorry on the one hand and yet I own that in school time I can scarcely undertake anything.

149

The winter, though much less severe in Ireland than in England, tried me more than any yet; half killed me; and leaves me languishing. Especially it has attacked my eyes, but perhaps this effect will pass off. The weather is now of a summer mildness.

I have done some part of a book on Pindar's metres and Greek metres in general and metre in general and almost on art in general and wider still, but that I shall ever get far on with it or, if I do, sail through all the rocks and shoals that lie before me I scarcely dare to hope and yet I do greatly desire, since the thoughts are well worth preserving: they are a solid foundation for criticism. What becomes of my verses I care little, but about things like this, what I write or could write on philosophical matters, I do; and the reason of the difference is that the verses stand or fall by their simple selves and, though by being read they might do good, by being unread they do no harm; but if the other things are unsaid right they will be said by somebody else wrong, and that is what will not let me rest.

I was at Xmas and New Year down with some kind people in Co. Kildare,[1] where I happened to see the portrait of two beautiful young persons, a brother and sister, living in the neighbourhood. It so much struck me that I began an elegy in Gray's metre,[2] but being back here I cannot go on with it. However I must see if I can enclose you a copy of the part done.

Have you heard of any great admirers of *Mano* or your other poems since *Mano* came out, by letter or otherwise? I set up a little Propaganda for Bridges' muse here lately, distributing, with commendations, the copies he sent me; also I have got a lady to compose her Doctorate-of-Music diploma work to his *Elegy on a Lady whom Grief* etc; and I tell people of you when I can put in a word. But it seems one can do little in this distracted globe and one is inclined to let things alone.

I have made the acquaintance of the young and ingenuous poetess Miss Kate Tynan,[3] a good creature and very graceful

---

[1] The Cassidys, of Monastereven.   [2] *Poems*, 54 (unfinished).
[3] Afterwards Mrs. Hinkson (1861–1931).

writer, highly and indeed somewhat too highly praised by a wonderful, perhaps alarming, unanimity of the critics; for the truth is she is not exactly an original 'fountain in a shady grove' (the critics would not be standing all round her so soon if she were), but rather a sparkling townfountain in public gardens and draws her water from other sources. She half knows this herself and lately wrote me a letter which for various reasons I am slow to answer and as long as I do not I cannot help telling myself very barbarously that I have stopped *her* jaw at any rate.

Jan. 29—Bridges says he has three works on hand. Like 'Young Copperfield' (according to Steerforth), he is going it.

Believe me your affectionate friend

GERARD M. HOPKINS S.J.

XXXIX

University College, St. Stephen's Green, Dublin. June 18 1887

MY DEAR FRIEND,—I have just begun my examining and shall be hard at it for weeks, a weary task indeed, but I must just let you know of (though that you perhaps will already; at any rate I wish to speak of it) an admiring notice of your *Lyrical Poems* in today's *Academy.*[1] It quotes all *the Spirit Wooed* and says it is 'an ode which takes rank with the finest in English'. After that he [the critic] makes further discoveries. There is an 'Ode to Fancy' which haunts him; there are songs which sing themselves; there are lines scattered all about which seem to interpret theories he once read about the province of the 'imagination' in poetry.

'Morning . . . claspèd hands.'

Indeed, he would not like to be asked too suddenly why this is all only minor poetry, as it must be since he is writing only a

[1] About a column (mainly quotation) is given to the book. G. M. H. gives the gist of it. R. B. added a footnote to this letter: 'The Academy Rev. ment[d] in this letter was by H. Beeching Rector of Yattendon who knew of the poems thro' me.'

minor review of it'. (The couplet 'morning' etc seems to be quoted in illustration of what goes just before.)

I was down at Monasterevan lately and managed to see the young lady of the Elegy, which however I have had no chance of continuing. She was in the earthquake on the Riviera and was much frightened.

Believe me your affectionate friend

GERARD M. HOPKINS.

XXXIX A

Warkworth Vicarage, Northumberland. 7 July 1887

MY DEAR FRIEND,—I have been long in acknowledging your kindnefs in writing to tell me of the Academy review. Thank you indeed. It was a pleasing incident.

You will now be in the midst, I suppose, of your Examination work: which is no doubt very severe & wearisome. Bridges has mentioned something of your music work, besides what you have told me yourself. How is that getting on? And do finish that Elegy.

Have you happened to see anything of the controversy on Gosse's book 'From Shakespeare to Pope', which shook the literary world (i.e. about half a dozen periodicals) some months ago?[1] I happen to have been reading the book. It is not good: but has some interesting points. Gosse is such a poor writer. If it were entirely rewritten, it might be made something of.

Some time or other I s.d be glad to have your opinion of a narrative poem in couplets, of the Byzantine times, that I have.[2] I will say more about it when I send it: which may not be for months.

I expect Bridges here this month, perhaps next week.

I am your affec.te friend

R. W. DIXON

[1] See vol. i, pp. 242–3.   [2] *The Story of Eudocia*; see p. 154.

XL

University College, St. Stephen's Green, Dublin. Dec. 22 1887

MY DEAR FRIEND,—It is long since I wrote to you, and I wonder why I should stint myself in one of the best pleasures of life. Bridges has a little daughter, I dare say you have heard; born on the 6th, I think. The weather, which has been wild but not dark or cold with us, has now turned to a sharp bright frost: I hope you do not find this, as you used to do at Carlisle, too searching. Tomorrow I am going down to my friends at Monasterevan in Co. Kildare, the scene of many misadventures (not to me) and now of the poisoning of the hounds, which threatens to put an end altogether to hunting in all that neighbourhood and with it to Punchestown races—what would mean on the whole the withdrawal of a great deal of money from the country. But that is how we live now and with fervour cut off our nose to revenge ourselves on our face.

I enclose two sonnets,[1] works of infinite, of over great contrivance, I am afraid, to the annulling in the end of the right effect. They have also too much resemblance to each other; but they were conceived at the same time. They are of a 'robustious' sort and perhaps 'Tom's Garland' approaches bluster and will remind you of Mr. Podsnap with his back to the fire. They are meant for, and cannot properly be taken in without, emphatic recitation; which nevertheless is not an easy performance.

I have Blake's poems by me. Some of them much remind me of yours. The best are of an exquisite freshness and lyrical inspiration, but there is mingled with the good work a great deal of rubbish, want of sense, and some touches of ribaldry and wickedness.

I cannot find your last letter, in which I think you spoke of shewing me some new poems. I should greatly like to read them; but I could not do so, I am afraid, with the closeness

---

[1] *Poems*, 42 and 43 (*Harry Ploughman*).

which is needed for serviceable criticism. I ought to have written about this before.

I thought I might copy some more sonnets, but they seem not quite ready and time runs. I cannot get my Elegy finished, but I hope in a few days to see the hero and heroine of it, which may enable me (or quite the reverse; perhaps that: it is not well to come too near things).

Believe me your affectionate friend

GERARD M. HOPKINS.

Dec. 23 1887. The post is gone. I wish you a very happy Christmas and new year.

I am at work on a great choral fugue! I can hardly believe it.

XLI

University College, St. Stephen's Green, Dublin. July 29 1888

MY DEAR FRIEND,—It is now weeks since your poem of Eudocia[1] was sent to me and I thank you very much for it. But it found me (as I still am, but see daylight) very very busy. (It is killing work to examine a nation.) At first I thought only to acknowledge it; then I began a longer letter of criticism, but it miscarried and then I could not begin again. The present must be betwixt the too little and too much.

I admired it, as I need scarcely say, throughout, but still, I can hardly tell why, read it with less of a distinct relish than I commonly read you—either the subject seemed somewhat chosen at haphazard and so to have been worked at with less enthusiasm, or that I felt more sympathy for Pulcheria than you do, or whatever the reason. I think it would be caviare to the general and the mastery of the style would be easily missed even by critics (as by the *Saturday*[2] it was).

---

[1] The Story of / Eudocia & her Brothers. / by / Richard Watson Dixon / Printed by H. Daniel, Fellow of / Worcester College: Oxford / 1888. Pp. vi. 35. 50 copies printed.

[2] See vol. i, p. 275, footnote 3, and vol. i, NOTE Y.

I can only mention a few points at random (I am writing from Milltown Park and the book is at the Green) which I especially admire or which I demur to. I am struck for instance by the feeling for the tragedy that is kneaded up in human life which your writing always displays, without effort and in any natural incident of the story. I admire the portrait of Theodosius drawn with disapproval but without any satire and appearing in the dialogue advantageously as a dignified gentleman and a fine mind, his weakness being then thrown into the background. The scene between him and the empress is a beautiful and subtle conception, it seems to me, and the waywardness of 'Or ate it—as thou wilt' a great and melancholy stroke. The scarcely perceptible touch of vanity in reminding Pulcheria that he had had to point a detail out to her is interesting. I much admire the thoroughly illustrative image of the fountain with half diverted source and the picture of Eudocia white as her tablets; also her answer 'Sir, I have thought of this' as delicately hitting the position of one who consents to a sort of intrigue without loss of candour or dignity. Also the incident of the desperate return to the river growing louder and louder in its bed, and of the two arrows. Also Eudocia declaiming to the air. You will I hope see that your strokes do not miss, or not all of them.

I feel a certain fault of construction (in a drama none, but less defensible in a narrative) in making Theodosius give the apple to Eudocia's brother in the forest and make all his appointments then and there and then be killed next minute, this being an unlikely concentration of events, and on the other hand that the news of it should not have reached Eudocia till her brother came with the apple. Can this be in the history?

Metrically I find some fault. I see no good in dropping a syllable (that is in giving a superfluous syllable) a few times at a stop. It is lawful and even effective in dramatic verse, and of course I know I often do it myself, but then on a very different rhythm and scheme of scanning; but in smooth narrative, in couplets, that highly polished metre, and for private reading

I think it needless and faulty and that it puts the reader out. However it is a very small matter.

Making *apple* and *arrow* in Chaucerian style one syllable has a quaint charm, the charm of learned archaism; still I think it wrong, and inconsistent with the rest of the scansion. In no modern pronunciation of English could *apple*, I think, be mono-syllabic (except of course if a vowel followed and the *e* were swallowed—like *appl'* and *pear*). *Arrow* on the other hand might here in Ireland become a diphthong, the *r* before a vowel being not trilled or rolled as in England but burred or 'furred' and half lost, so that the sound is like *ah-o* and almost *ow* (they say 'the marge and buryal of an Ornge barster in Meryon Square', that is, *the marriage and burial* etc); and nearly this, no doubt, was Chaucer's sound; but you cannot well take your ground on that. And then, as above, the rest is not of a piece.

I make the same objection of inconsistency to a remarkable condensation or hurrying of syllables in 'to have avoided' some-where: the line is, to be sure, to me who have the key, pleasing; but to others it will appear ever so much too long and you have scarcely prepared the reader for it. Instead of an instance it is an exception and instead of a last flourish an abrupt freak.

Lastly to touch on what is universal and woven into the whole, though I always hold that your archaism is the most beautiful (as also I believe the most learned) archaism of any modern poet's, the only one that is of itself a living beauty in the style, still I cannot think even so that it is right: I look on the whole *genus* as vicious.

Which reminds me of Swinburne's *Locrine*.[1] I rēad very little modern poetry, however I rēad that. It is scarcely to be called a play and the characterisation is youthful (Madan for instance is quite *cousu avec de fil blanc*; he makes his points like the Governor of Tilbury Fort or Sir Christopher Hatton in the *Critic*); but for music of words and the mastery and employment of a con-sistent and distinctive poetic diction, a style properly so called, it is extraordinary. But the diction is Elisabethan or nearly:

---

[1] Published in 1887.

not one sentence is properly modern, except where there could in no case be any difference to be made. I shd. think it could only be in Persian or some other eastern language that a poetical dialect so ornate and continuously beautiful could be found. But words only are only words.

What a preposterous summer! It is raining now: when is it not? However there was one windy bright day between floods last week: fearing for my eyes, with my other rain of papers, I put work aside and went out for the day, and conceived a sonnet. Otherwise my muse has long put down her carriage and now for years 'takes in washing' The laundry is driving a great trade now.

I hope your health is restored.

Believe me your affectionate friend

GERARD M. HOPKINS.

Please write more odes. The ode 'Thou goest more and more'[1] seems to me one of the very grandest ever written in anything.

July 30 1888.

I have done some more of my elegy and hope to finish it.

[1] *Ode on Advancing Age, Lyrical Poems,* 1887 (*S.P.*, pp. 132–5).

APPENDIX I

A PRAYER[1]

ALMIGHTY and Everlasting God, from whom and through whom and in whom all things are, from whose hand we, with all the world besides, every moment take our being, we appear before thee humbly to acknowledge that thou art the one true God, boundless in thy power, wisdom, goodness, the maker of all things made, the watchful witness and just judge of all things done. Not only this, which all nature speaks to and which is written in our hearts of thee, but we acknowledge too and firmly believe those secrets of thy being which man could never know of till thou didst of thyself reveal them, sending into the world thy only begotten son Jesus Christ our Lord, who being God is thy equal and being made man became thy servant and for our salvation died upon the cross. With thee and with him, both from thee and him proceeding, we acknowledge the Holy Ghost, three equal persons in one nature and godhead, according as the same Christ thy son at his last leaving of the earth proclaimed and bid his followers teach men everywhere. Whatever there is more than this, O thou that art truth's and wisdom's self, which thou wouldst have us to believe and to confess, so far as it has come or shall come to our knowledge we do believe and do confess, bowing to thy obedience our minds with their unwisdom and shortsightedness.

But thou, O God, madest us to serve thee, in our thoughts to reverence, and with our lips or by our deeds to praise thee; and with sorrow we own against ourselves that whereas we should have glorified thy majesty we have grievously come short of thy glory; nay worse, that we have been thy rebels and many many times in small things and in great broken thy holy law and not kept thy commandments. We are ashamed, we look at ourselves and thee and are confounded. We wither at thy rebuke, we faint at thy frown, we tremble at thy power and threatened punishments. To offence we have added ingratitude, because for these same sins thy son had died; therefore we have despised his death. But have mercy, O Lord, have mercy on us sinners. We repent of our sins, we wish they were undone; they cannot be undone, but thou canst pardon them; we humbly hope to be forgiven. And though we cannot ask for ever to be free from all the faults which, daily, human frailty falls into, yet we do hope and, with thy seasonable help afforded, earnestly

---

[1] See vol. i, p. 183. The MS., which has no title, is found on pp. 2–5 of A, and it is indexed by R. B. as 'a prayer written for protestants'. In A is also found another prayer, by G. M. H., presumably a translation.

purpose never wilfully and with full malice to offend thee; and, that in this we may not mock thee with our promises, we add this promise too, not without necessity to venture into those occasions which either we forsee or sad experience has taught us will to us be fatal or dangerous. Yet if, which do thou forbid, these promises of ours were to be broken, however deeply and however often, still we should hope for fresh grace to repent and be forgiven. For thou desirest not the sinner's death, but that he should be converted and live. Our better hope, built on the promise of thy availing help, is never more to sin against thee, but henceforth to live as in thy sight and in the doing of thy service, the end that we were made for and our bounden duty; living thus, at our deaths to hear thy sentence of mercy; and, meeting with thy mercy, to see thy face for ever.

But we remember, O our good God, that, here too and not here-after only, thou art the heart's comfort and the fulfilment of the soul's desire. We wish to love thee as, both for thyself and for thy goodness to us, thou dost deserve to be loved and hast commanded us to love thee. For if our hearts are in feeling cold, yet that love we can give to thee which to thee as lord and sovereign belongs, namely the keeping of thy commandments and the doing of thy will, even where it is against our own, thy holy and perfect will against our easily misguided ones. And in the bond of this same charity we for thy sake love our neighbours, all men, wishing them well, not ill; purposing to do them good, not evil; forgiving also all who have offended us, as we by thee hope to be forgiven. This and all our prayers we offer through the merits of thy son Jesus Christ our Lord, who liveth and reigneth with thee and the Holy Ghost one God world without end. Amen.

APPENDIX II

LETTERS CONTRIBUTED TO *NATURE* BY G. M. H.

A

THE phenomenon described by M. Dechevrens as often witnessed in China, I have several times seen in this country, namely, beams or spokes in the eastern sky about sunset, springing from a point due opposite to the sun. The appearance is not very strongly marked, and I used to think I must have been mistaken, till I came to see the true explanation, which was the same as that furnished by your correspondent.

There seems no reason why the phenomenon should not be common, and perhaps if looked out for it would be found to be. But who looks east at sunset? Something in the same way everybody has seen the rainbow; but the solar halo, which is really commoner, few people, not readers of scientific works, have ever seen at all. The appearance in question is due to cloud-shadows in an unusual perspective and in a clear sky; now shadow may not only be seen carried by misty, mealy, dusty, or smoky air near the ground, but even on almost every bright day, by seemingly clear air high overhead. Therefore, if this sunset phenomenon is much commoner in China, there must one would think, be some other reason for it than that the sky of England is not heavily charged enough with vapour to carry shadow. Rather it is too much charged, and the edge of the shadow becomes lost with distance and with the thickening of the air towards the horizon before the convergence of the beams eastwards is marked enough to catch the eye.

I may remark that things common at home have sometimes first been remarked abroad. The stars in snow were first observed in the polar regions; it was thought that they only arose there, but now everyone sees them with the naked eye on his coatsleeve.

GERARD HOPKINS.

Stonyhurst College.[1]

B

SHADOW-BEAMS IN THE EAST AT SUNSET[2]

The phenomenon of beams of shadow meeting in the east at sunset, treated of in the pages of NATURE some months since (at which time you did me the honour of inserting a letter of mine), was beauti-

[1] The issue of 16 November 1882. The letter, which appears under the heading 'A Curious Halo', is a comment on a letter from Father Marc Dechevrens.
[2] The issue of 15 November 1883.

fully witnessed here today and yesterday. Both days were unusually clear; there was, nevertheless, a 'body' in the air, without which the propagation of the beams could not take place. Yesterday the sky was striped with cirrus cloud like swaths of a hayfield; only in the east there was a bay or reach of clear blue sky, and in this the shadow-beams appeared, slender, colourless, and radiating every way like a fan wide open. This lasted from 3.30 to about 4.30. Today the sky was cloudless, except for a low bank in the west; in the east was a 'cast' of blue mist, from which sprang alternate broad bands of rose colour and blue, slightly fringed. I was not able to look for them till about 4.30, when the sun was down, and they soon faded. I have not before seen this appearance so far north, but on the south coast, where I first saw it, I think it might often be witnessed. It is merely an effect of perspective, but a strange and beautiful one.

GERARD HOPKINS.

Stonyhurst College, November 12.

C

The body of evidence now brought in from all parts of the world must, I think, by this time have convinced Mr. Piazzi Smyth that the late sunrises and sunsets do need some explanation, more particular than he was willing to give them. With your leave I should like to point out from my own observations and those of others that, 'given a clear sky' and the other conditions put by Mr. Smyth, the sunrises and sunsets of other days, however bright and beautiful, have *not* given any such effects as were witnessed, to take an instance, here on Sunday night, December 16th. I shall speak chiefly of the sunsets.[1]

(1) *These sunsets differ from others, first in their time and their place or quarter.* Sunset proper is, I suppose, the few minutes between the first dipping and the last disappearance of the sun's disk below the true horizon; the pageant or phenomena we call sunset, however, includes a great deal that goes on before and after this. The remarkable and specific features of the late sunsets have not been before or

---

[1] See vol. i, p. 202. This letter, contained in the issue of 3 January 1884, is part of a considerable correspondence in *Nature* on 'The Remarkable Sunsets', and is prefixed by an editorial note on the evidence about them and their cause that was rapidly being collected. Krakatoa, a small volcanic island between Java and Sumatra, a crater partly submerged in the sea, erupted 26–28 August 1883, blowing most of the island to pieces, and several new islets were formed from the debris. For some months afterwards there were very fine sunsets, due to the reflection downwards of the sun's rays from the upper atmosphere after sunset, this upper air over most of the world being affected by volcanic dust.

at sunset proper; they have been after-glows, and have lasted long, very long, after. To take instances from your number of the 13th ult., Mr. F. A. R. Russell notices that on November 28th, the sun having set at 3.55, one after-glow lasted till 5.10, and was then succeeded by another 'reaching high above the horizon'. The day before he mentions the after-glow as lasting to 5.20. On the 29th a 'FOREglow' is reported as seen in London from 5.30 to 7.30, that is more than two hours before sunrise, which was at 7.43. On December 1st, sunset being at 3.53, Mr. Russell observed an after-glow till 5.35; on December 4th the first dawn at 6.5, the sun rising at 7.50; the next day dawn at the same time, sunrise 7.51; that evening, sunset being at 3.50, he observed not a glow only but 'spokes of rays from the glowing bank' at 4.45, that is to say, sunbeams, visible in the shape of sunbeams, 55 minutes after sunset. Mr. Johnston-Lavis speaks of the after-glow at Naples as *at a maximum* an hour after sunset. Here at Stonyhurst on December 16th, the sun having set at 3.49, the glow was observed till 5.50. Now winter dawns and after-glows do not last from an hour to two hours, and still less so day after day, as these have done. The recent sunrises and sunsets then differ from others in duration.

They differ also in the quarter of the heavens where they are seen. The after-glows are not low lingering slips of light skirting the horizon, but high up in the sky, sometimes in the zenith.

I have further remarked that the deepest of the after-glow is in the south, whereas the sun below the horizon, is then northing. I see that other observers take notice of the same.

(2) *They differ in their periodic action or behaviour.* The flushes of crimson and other colours after ordinary sunsets are irregular, not the same nor at the same time for two days together; for they depend upon the accidental shapes and sizes and densities of the cloud-banks or vapour-banks the sun is entering or freeing himself from, which vary and can never be alike from day to day. But these glows or flushes are noticed to be periodic before sunrise and after sunset. Mr. Russell furnishes exact estimates of the intervals of time, which he finds to be the same day after day.

(3) *They differ in the nature of the glow, which is both intense and lustreless,* and that both in the sky and in the earth. The glow is intense, this is what strikes everyone; it has prolonged the daylight, and optically changed the season; it bathes the whole sky, it is mistaken for the reflection of a great fire; at the sundown itself and southwards from that on December 4, I took a note of it as more like inflamed flesh than the lucid reds of ordinary sunsets. On the same evening the fields facing west glowed as if overlaid with yellow wax.

But it is also lustreless. A bright sunset lines the clouds so that their brims look like gold, brass, bronze, or steel. It fetches out those dazzling flecks and spangles which people call fish-scales. It gives to a mackerel or dappled cloudrack the appearance of quilted crimson silk, or a ploughed field glazed with crimson ice. These effects may have been seen in the late sunsets, but they are not the specific after-glow; that is, without gloss or lustre.

The two things together, that is intensity of light and want of lustre, give to objects on the earth the peculiar illumination which may be seen in studios and other well-like rooms, and which itself affects the practice of painters and may be seen in their works, notably Rembrandt's, disguising or feebly showing the outlines and distinctions of things, but fetching out white surfaces and coloured stuffs with a rich and inward and seemingly self-luminous glow.

(4) *They differ in the regularity of their colouring.* Four colours in particular have been noticeable in these after-glows, and in a fixed order of time and place—orange, lowest and nearest the sundown; above this, and broader, green; above this, broader still, a variable red, ending in being crimson; above this a faint lilac. The lilac disappears; the green deepens, spreads and encroaches on the orange; and the red deepens, spreads, and encroaches on the green, till at last one red, varying downwards from crimson to scarlet or orange fills the west and south. The four colours I have named are mentioned in Lieut. G. N. Bittleson's letter from Umballa: 'The sun goes down as usual and it gets nearly dark, and then a bright red and yellow and green and purple blaze comes in the sky and makes it lighter again.' I suppose the yellow here spoken of to be an orange yellow, and the purple to be what I have above called lilac.

Ordinary sunsets have not this order; this, so to say, fixed and limited palette. The green in particular, is low down when it appears. There is often a trace of olive between the sundown and the higher blue sky, but it never developes, that I remember, into a fresh green.

(5) *They differ in the colours themselves, which are impure and not of the spectrum.* The first orange and the last crimson flush are perhaps pure, or nearly so, but the two most remarkable glows, the green and the red, are not. The green is between an apple-green or pea-green (which are pure greens) and an olive (which is tertiary colour): it is vivid and beautiful, but not pure. The red is very impure, and not evenly laid on. On the 4th it appeared brown, like a strong light behind tortoiseshell, or Derbyshire alabaster. It has been well compared to the colour of incandescent iron. Sometimes it appears like a mixture of chalk with sand and muddy earths. The pigments for it would be ochre and Indian red.

Now the yellows, oranges, crimsons, purples, and greens of bright sunsets are beautifully pure. Tertiary colours may of course also be found in certain cases and places.

(6) *They differ in the texture of the coloured surfaces*, which are neither distinct cloud of recognised make nor yet translucent mediums. Mr. Russell's observations should here be read. I have further noticed streamers, fine ribbing or mackerelling, and other more curious textures, the colour varying with the texture.

In ordinary sunsets the yellows and greens and the lower reds look like glass, or coloured liquids, as pure as the blue. Other colours, or these in other parts, are distinct flushes or illuminations of cloud or landscape.

I subjoin an account of the sunset of the 16th, which was here very remarkable, from my own observations and those of one of the observatory staff.

A bright glow had been round the sun all day and became more remarkable towards sunset. It then had a silvery or steely look, with soft radiating streamers and little colour; its shape was mainly elliptical, the slightly longer axis being vertical; the size about 20° from the sun each way. There was a pale gold colour, brightening and fading by turns for ten minutes as the sun went down. After the sunset the horizon was, by 4.10, lined a long way by a glowing tawny light, not very pure in colour and distinctly textured in hummocks, bodies like a shoal of dolphins, or in what are called gadroons, or as the Japanese conventionally represent waves. The glowing vapour above this was as yet colourless; then this took a beautiful olive or celadon green, not so vivid as the previous day's, and delicately fluted; the green belt was broader than the orange, and pressed down on and contracted it. Above the green in turn appeared a red glow, broader and burlier in make; it was softly brindled, and in the ribs or bars the colour was rosier, in the channels where the blue of the sky shone through it was a mallow colour. Above this was a vague lilac. The red was first noticed 45° above the horizon, and spokes or beams could be seen in it, compared by one beholder to a man's open hand. By 4.45 the red had driven out the green, and, fusing with the remains of the orange, reached the horizon. By that time the east, which had a rose tinge, became of a duller red, compared to sand; according to my observation, the ground of the sky in the east was green or else tawny, and the crimson only in the clouds. A great sheet of heavy dark cloud, with a reefed or puckered make, drew off the west in the course of the pageant: the edge of this and the smaller pellets of cloud that filed across the bright field of the sundown caught a livid green. At 5 the red in the west was fainter, at 5.20 it became notably rosier and livelier; but it was never of a pure rose. A faint dusky blush was left as late as 5.30, or later. While these changes were going on in the sky, the landscape of Ribblesdale glowed with a frowning brown.

The two following observations seem to have to do with the same phenomena and their causes. For some weeks past on fine bright days, when the sun has been behind a big cloud and has sent up (perspectively speaking) the dark crown or paling of beams of shadow in such cases commonly to be seen, I have remarked, upon the ground of the sky, sometimes an amber, sometimes a soft rose colour, instead of the usual darkening of the blue. Also on moonlight nights, and particularly on December 14, a sort of brown or muddy cast, never before witnessed, has been seen by more than one observer, in the sky.

GERARD HOPKINS.

Stonyhurst College, December 21, 1883.

G. M. H. AS ARTIST AND MUSICIAN

G. M. H. had considerable gifts as an artist, and while at school and Oxford devoted much time to sketching, both in England and while visiting the Continent. Certain of his sketch-books are extant, and will be found described below. The most finished work in them shows the influence of Ruskin and the Pre-Raphaelites. The only 'imaginative' drawing of his that I have seen is the remarkable Blake-like heading to the manuscript of his early poem, *A Vision of the Mermaids* (1862), of which a facsimile is available (O.U.P. 1929). The three sketch-books that I have examined measure $4\frac{1}{2}$ in. × 3 in., and may thus be described:

A. Inscribed: 'Gerard M. Hopkins. March 11th 1862. Esse quam videri.' Nearly all the sketches are in pencil. They range in date from 12 March 1862 to 8 August 1863, and chiefly illustrate a holiday spent in the Isle of Wight. They include landscapes, trees, flowers, cloud effects, and one study of a wave. Several of them are delicately, even elaborately, finished; but the most striking in this respect is a pen and ink drawing, dated April–July 1862, called 'Dandelion, Hemlock and Ivy. The field, Blunt House, Croydon', an exquisite tracery of stem, flower, and leaf, attractive in its intricacy of detail. With it may be mentioned an unfinished pencil sketch of a similar kind, and a Birket Foster-like view of North Road, Highgate. Two studies of clouds have the appropriate colours written on them.

B. Inscribed: 'Gerard Hopkins. 1863.' This carries on from A with work done at Shanklin in September; and the last drawing is of 5 October 1865. There are a few sketches made near Oxford, one in Wales, and a few in Devonshire. These chiefly deal with landscape or trees. There are two attempts at drawing men—the first is unsuccessful (face scribbled over), and the other shows a figure lying on cushions in a punt reading a book which, with the hands, hides his face.

C. Inscribed: 'G. M. Hopkins, Aug. 15, '66.' This contains a few pencil studies of trees and leaves ranging in date from 16 August 1866 to June 1868, but is chiefly devoted to rough suggestions of Alpine scenery made during July 1868.

In addition, Mr. Humphry House tells me that there is one sketch-book in the possession of the Society of Jesus which contains nothing of unusual interest, and no work different in style from that mentioned above. The Diaries 'are intermittently illustrated, but the sketches are only of interest with reference to the context'.

The impression left by this work (except for the early drawing) is in contrast to that conveyed by the poems. The attraction lies in the careful, sustained observation of detail and beautiful finish rather than in bold grasp or freshness of approach. Here is charm, not strength; acceptance, not discovery: and the charm has in it small sign of future growth.

As will be seen from his *Letters*, G. M. H. became more and more interested in music, and despite his lack of technical training obviously felt that he could make a contribution of importance to that art based on new theories. So absorbed is he in this pursuit, so enthusiastic about his work in it, that the reader of his poetry expects to find that he has brought to music a similar genius and freshness of approach. This seems, in the main, not to be so, on the evidence of what material survives for judgement. Yet, as will be seen, one or two of his compositions are noteworthy.

Musicians will be able to form their own conclusions on the value of his theories. My purpose here is to gather together opinions that have been expressed by musicians on what scattered work survives. There is no certainty that it is his best work, though a good deal of what he mentions in the *Letters* has now been accounted for. (It is perhaps well to recall that Sir Robert Stewart, to whom he went for advice, evidently thought him a stubbornly wrong-headed amateur.)

These opinions run thus:

(1) Dr. Stewart, organist of Magdalen College, Oxford, who has seen only what music and occasional references are contained in the *Letters* themselves, says:

'Though his technical training was admittedly slender, he seems to have been fond of exhibiting his melodies in canon, and defended stoutly his harmonization against the criticisms of the experts. There is evidence in his letters of the urge to composition, and that he took a special delight in any points of originality or novelty in his work. Indeed, he almost claims that his harmonic treatment of Gregorian melody was more adventurous than purists would have approved, as if he were jumping a generation and anticipating the modern modal style, though there is no extant example to justify the supposition. But his artistic attitude was that of reaching forward beyond the restrictions of the contrapuntists of his time.'

Appendix III

(2) Mr. Gerard Hopkins sent me an exercise in counterpoint and two settings of songs (*a*) *Wayward Water* (R. W. D.'s 'Sky that rollest ever'), which was perhaps not in G. M. H.'s handwriting. (*b*) A few bars in pencil of 'Who is Sylvia?'. An expert reported these to be 'musically without interest'.

(3) Mr. Humphry House, who has investigated G. M. H.'s papers in Ireland, writes:

'I have seen several musical exercises of his and referred them to competent musicians who report that they are all the most elementary work which would have been undertaken by a beginner in Composition. The settings of songs are judged to be very ordinary, and rather surprisingly showing no marked talent or even eccentricity.'

(4) While this book was passing through the press, another search by Miss Grace Hopkins, for possible poems of R. W. D. copied by G. M. H., resulted also in the discovery of a small bundle of G. M. H.'s music, perhaps the most important body of his work in this kind found so far. This has been examined by Mr. J. Dykes Bower, organist of Durham Cathedral, and his report on it follows. (It should be understood that Mr. Dykes Bower has seen no other music by G. M. H.)

'The MS. music of Hopkins that I have seen may be classified thus:

(*a*) A setting of "Sky that rollest ever", words by Canon Dixon. This is found on three sheets, the first containing the setting of the first verse only with an accompaniment by Miss Grace Hopkins; the second the melody for three verses, each verse being slightly different, with a sketch for an accompaniment to the second verse; the third the tune of the first verse with a canon at the octave below, which, however, breaks down after a few bars. The tune is of no particular interest.

(*b*) Two settings—melody only—of "Who is Sylvia?". Of these one, in C major, is devoid of interest. The other, in F major, has a graceful tune and is rather reminiscent in style of English songs of the eighteenth century. Each verse, however, starts with a glaring false accent.

(*c*) A setting—melody only—of "Fallen Rain", words by Canon Dixon. This is a tune of real distinction, and is quoted here. Its most interesting features are: the beauty of the refrain, "Why am I cast down?"; the effective cross rhythms; the flattened seventh in the twenty-second bar suggestive of modal influence; the fine climax on high A flat in the thirty-fifth bar; the falling sevenths at the words "I fall and die"; and the use of a quarter-tone in the thirty-ninth bar, and its notation—a flat turned backwards. Quarter-tones were used in ancient Greek music and it was doubtless Hopkins's acquaintance with Greek music that suggested the experiment. In view of present-day experiments in quarter-tones this passage is interesting.

(*d*) A setting—melody only—of the Ballad from the *Winter's Tale*, "Get you hence, for I must go". This attractive tune again shows very clearly the influence of Greek modal music. It seems almost to be single-toned music, defying all attempts to harmonize it.

(*e*) A setting—voice part and accompaniment—of "Done to death by slanderous tongues", from *Much Ado About Nothing*. This is a poor tune, badly harmonized.

(*f*) A setting, with pianoforte accompaniment, of Campbell's "Battle of the Baltic" (first two stanzas) for two choirs singing in unison, the first choir consisting of the British, the second of the Danes. The second stanza is in the form of a ground bass (mis-named by Hopkins Basso Continuo) on an excellent subject

which undergoes skilful rhythmical variation on each of the ten repetitions. This composition has many ideas, but Hopkins's inadequate knowledge of harmony prevented his making really effective use of them.'

POEMS BY R. W. DIXON COPIED BY G. M. HOPKINS

THESE poems fall into two groups:

(a) Those chosen from *Christ's Company* and *Historical Odes*. The writing is of one period (see vol. ii, p. 1). They are: St. Paul, St. John [stanza xxxii, l. 5 has the following pencil note: Shd. the line be Beside the rainbow, blessed?" She—"Behold], Love's Consolation, To Summer, Dream, Waiting, Ballad, To Shadow, Mother and Daughter, Sonnet ['Give me the darkest corner of a cloud'], Dawning, Inscience, Song ['The feathers of the willow'], The Sole Survivor, Sunset.

(b) Those that were copied at a later date, and evidently from manuscript, since there are small changes from the printed version. These poems are: Ode on Conflicting Claims, Nature and Man, Death and Victory, The Spirit Wooed, Life and Death, The Secret Execution (till now unpublished, so far as I know), O ubi? Nusquam [with this note: 'Written, I suppose, in memory of his wife. The repetition of a word in the second lines is an afterthought and has not been executed throughout.' This repetition disappears in the printed version: e.g. st. 4, l. 2 in manuscript reads—'So many fields, such meadows, meadows vast.'], Winter will Follow [after which comes the note: 'The three Songs *Fallen Rain, Sky that rollest ever,* and *Does the South Wind* I know by heart and can write down at any time'], Fallen Rain, [Wayward Water], [Ruffling Wind]. The last two poems have this note: 'The bracketed titles are mine: Canon Dixon gave no titles to these two poems.'

These have been printed, except

THE SECRET EXECUTION[2]

I heard thy foot that stept
And broad awake I leapt:
Wouldst murder me whilst I slept?

I see thee there full well:
This darkness as of hell
Bears sparkles in its well.

Lo, thou art stepping now
And balancing to and fro
As if to a fiddle and bow;

---

[1] See vol. ii, Preface, p. vii.   [2] See vol. ii. p. 64.

³ A soundless fiddle and bow
Thou steppest and steppest, I trow,
And good time keepest thou.

I see thee from hair to toe:
To a soundless fiddle and bow
Thou steppest and steppest, I trow.

And turning back thy head,
Thou pointest a knife instead
Of the edge of an eye that's afraid.

My wrists are laid in one link
Of the chain: it shall not clink
To tell in what corner I shrink.

My wrists are drawn down by the chain:
Silently, spite of the pain,
To burst it in sunder I strain.

If I can but make shift
The iron from the floor to rift
And my arms o'er my head to lift.

¹ Read *To a* (note by G. M. H.).

ADDITIONAL NOTES
VOLUME II

NOTE A, *page* 1. A review, running to seven columns, that took pride of place. It concludes: 'But our sense of gratitude to Canon Dixon for giving us a work of so much value would outweigh far more serious drawbacks than these [minor peculiarities of expression and spelling]. It is seldom, indeed, that a book contains so much evidence alike of independent thought and of conscientious labour. The result must surely be to aid largely in displacing those crude superficial views of the great religious movement of the sixteenth century, which the careless uncritical pen of Burnet vindicated to the satisfaction of an age that believed in the Popish Plot.'

NOTE B, *page* 13.

How beautiful is night!
A dewy freshness fills the silent air;
No mist obscures, nor cloud, nor speck, nor stain,
Breaks the serene of heaven:
In full-orb'd glory yonder Moon divine
Rolls through the dark blue depths.
Beneath her steady ray
The desert-circle spreads,
Like the round ocean, girdled with the sky.
How beautiful is night!

NOTE C, *page* 16. For Thomas Gordon Hake (1809–95), physician, poet, and friend of Rossetti, see Richard Garnett's article in *D.N.B.*; the article and selections by Thomas Bayne in *Poets and Poetry of the Century*, edited by A. H. Miles; and his own autobiography, *Memoirs of Eighty Years* (1892). A reproduction of Rossetti's portrait of him may be found in the selections from his poems made by Alice Meynell in 1894. *The Snake Charmer* (published in *New Symbols*, 1876), one of his best poems, is included in Miles's anthology and Mrs. Meynell's selection. It has power, interest, and pattern. *Legends of the Morrow* (1879) includes the much weaker *The Palmist*, greatly admired by Rossetti, who had favourably reviewed Hake's earlier works, *Madeleine* in the *Academy*, 1871, and *Parables and Tales* in the *Fortnightly Review*, 1873.

NOTE D, *page* 18. Part of Coleridge's note to *Christabel*:
' . . . the metre of the Christabel is not, properly speaking, irregular, though it may seem so from its being founded on a new principle: namely, that of counting in each line the accents, not the syllables. Though the latter may vary from seven to twelve, yet in each line the accents will be found to be only four. Nevertheless this occasional variation in number of syllables is not introduced wantonly, or for the mere ends of convenience, but in correspondence with some transition, in the nature of the imagery or passion.'

Additional Notes

NOTE E, *page* 42.

SPRING AND FALL:
to a young child

Márgarét, áre you gríeving
Over Goldengrove unleafing?
Léaves, líke the thíngs of mán, you
With your fresh thoughts care for, can you?
Áh! ás the héart grows ólder
It will come to such sights colder—
By and by, nor spare a sigh
Where worlds of wanwood, leafmeal, lie;
And yet you will weep and know why.
Now no matter, child, the name:
Sórrow's spríngs áre the sáme.
Nor mouth it, no nor mind expressed,
But héart héard of, ghóst guéssed:
It ís the blíght mán was bórn for,
It is Margaret you mourn for.

Lydiate, Lancashire. Sept. 1880

NOTE F, *page* 42.

BROTHERS

How lóvely is the⌢élder bróther's
Love, all laced in the⌢other's
Béing! I have wátched this wéll
Once, as my fortune fell.
Shrovetide, two years gone,
Our schoolboys' plays drew on
And a part was picked for John
The yóung one: féar, jóy
Ran a rével in the élder bóy.
Now the night come, all
Our company thronged the hall;
Henry, by the wall,
Beckoned me beside him;
I came where called and eyed him
And the play, though my play
Turned most on tender byplay.
For wrung all on love's rack,
All lost, my lad, in Jack,
Smiled, blushed, and bit his lip,
Or drove, with a diver's dip,
Clutched hands down through clasped knees—
True tokens tricks like these,
Old telltales with what stress
He hung on the⌢imp's success.

Additional Notes

Now the⌒óther was bráss-bóld:
He had no work to hold
His heart up at the strain;
Nay, rogueish ran the vein.
Two tedious acts were past;
Jack's call and cue at last;
When Henry, heart-forsook,
Dropped eyes and dared not look.'
Hárk! the háll rúng.
Dog, he did give tongue!
But Harry—in his hands he has flung
His tear-tricked cheeks of flame
Fσr fond love and for shame.
Ah nature, framed in fault,
There's comfort then, there's salt;
Naⴓre, bad, base, and blind,
Dearly, thou canst be kind—
There déarly thén, déarly
I'll cry thou canst be kind.

Hampstead. Aug. 1880

NOTE G, *page* 49. 'We should have been glad to speak in the same generally favourable terms of this as we did of the preceding part of the History; but one defect which we noticed—viz., the author's inadequate appreciation of character—comes out more strongly now than before. And this is one of the causes of his failure to grasp the nature of the changes inaugurated in the first two years of Edward's reign, beyond which the present volume does not reach.

'Our author appears to have formed no true conception of the characters of the principal agents in the changes of religion that were being gradually forced on the nation; neither, again, is he sufficiently acquainted with the literature of the period to appreciate the real state of the case. . . .

'Not only is Mr. Dixon entirely at sea as regards English politicians and divines, but he does not seem to understand the position of the foreigners whom Cranmer invited over to help him to establish unity among the divided sects of Protestantism. . . .'

The reviewer suggests authorities to consult, and a new orientation. There is throughout little praise.

NOTE H, *page* 77.

As an Eagle, half strength and half grace,
Most potent to face
Unwinking the splendour of light;
Harrying the East and the West,
Soaring aloft from our sight;

Yet one day or one night dropped to rest,
On the low common earth
Of his birth.

NOTE I, *page* 90. In his *Church History* (vol. ii, pp. 230–2), R. W. D. has interesting things to say about the establishment and influence of the Jesuits, 'a new religious order which was destined to exercise a greater influence on the course of human events than any similar organisation in the world, but less in England than in any other country'. He analyses the genius of the order, shows how it differs from others, and how it 'encouraged the development of the most various talents'. After naming some Jesuits famous in letters, he continues: 'But it has been remarked with truth that the Jesuits, with all their culture, cannot boast the greatest names in any department. Their system consumed them: and, after all, the end of their system was active and political, not intellectual. Literature owes far less to them than to the later Benedictines. Theology owes far less to them than to the Franciscans. . . .'

NOTE J, *page* 121. A long and mildly appreciative review of *Mano*, unsigned [Andrew Lang], in the *Saturday Review* of 8 Sept. 1883. Much of it is given up to a summary of the poem, with long quotations. The following passages, from the beginning and end, will give some idea of the temper of the judgement.

'Canon Dixon's earlier poems, known perhaps to few, were written when Mr. Morris was writing the *Defence of Guenevere*. They had the eccentricities, the obscurities, and several of the merits of that interesting volume of verse, which revived a neglected aspect of mediæval life and imagination. After a long silence (so far as verse is concerned) Canon Dixon again appears with a volume of poetry, a romantic narrative in *terza rima*. When Mr. Morris deserted lyrical for narrative poetry he chose first a Greek theme (romantically treated) in the *Life and Death of Jason*. Canon Dixon, on the other hand, remains constant to the Middle Ages. He has chosen for the period of his tale what we may regard as the very central darkness of· the "Dark Ages"—the gloomy later years of the tenth century, when men's hearts were failing them for fear and doubtfully expecting the advent of Christ or Antichrist. . . .

'Such is the story which must be read with leisure and attention to be enjoyed. It has the advantage of novelty, and at the same time lacks the clearness and charm of those old world fables which Mr. Morris has chosen to tell again in *Jason* and *The Earthly Paradise*. It is plain that *Mano* is the work of a refined, learned, and curious mind, full of knowledge and of sympathy, and moving in ancient times with the ease born of long familiarity. We have not tried to conceal what we think the faults of the poem— intricacy, prolixity, occasional obscurity. Except Joanna and Fergant, the characters are somewhat shadowy; even that of Mano is too laboured to be quite distinct. We need scarcely remark on the numerous archaistic expressions, "wan of ble", and the like, nor on such oddities as rhyming "archbishop" to "stop" and "drop" . . . But these wilful turns are blots so readily observed

Additional Notes

that we need not waste more criticism on faults so certain to be criticized. We have read Canon Dixon's poem, if not constantly with ease, yet often with pleasure, and always with sympathy and respect for work so well wrought and so original.'

NOTE K, *page* 126. G. M. H.'s remarks on R. W. D. are to be found on pp. 470–1 of A Manual / of / English Literature / Historical and Critical / . . . By / Thomas Arnold, M.A. / of Univ. Coll. Oxford / Fellow of the Royal University of Ireland, and Professor of English / Language and Literature in the University College / Stephen's Green, Dublin / Fifth Edition, Revised / 1885.

'Richard Watson Dixon, now vicar of Warkworth and hon. canon of Carlisle, was born at Islington, near London, in 1833, and educated at King Edward's School, Birmingham, and Pembroke College, Oxford. At Oxford he became the friend and colleague of William Morris, Burne-Jones, and others of the mediævalist school, to which, as a poet, he belongs. The chance reading of his earlier poems also won for him the friendship of D. G. Rossetti.

'He is engaged on a history of the Church of England on a great scale; of this three volumes have appeared. In verse he has published—in 1859, *Christ's Company, and other Poems*; in 1863, *Historical Odes* (on Marlborough, Wellington, Sir John Franklin, &c.); in 1883, *Mano* (his greatest work, a romance-epic in *terza rima*: Mano is a Norman knight put to death A.D. 1000, and the story, darkly and affectingly tragic, turns upon the date); in 1884, *Odes and Eclogues*.

'In his poems we find a deep thoughtfulness and earnestness, and a mind touched by a pathos of human life, of which *Mano* is, in a strange but a typical case, the likeness; noble but never highflown, sad without noise or straining—everything as it most reaches and comes home to man's heart. In particular he is a master of horror (see Mano's words about the nettles on his way to the stake) and pathos; of pathos so much that here it would be hard to name his rival. We find also the very rare gift of pure imagination, such as Coleridge had (see the song "Fallen Rain", and the one on the sky wooing the river). But he is likest and owes most to Keats, and his description and imagery are realised with a truth and splendour not less than Keats' own (see the scene of the nine lovers in *Love's Consolation*; the images of the quicksilver and of the heart fastened round with hair, *ibidem*). This richness of image, matched with the deep feeling which flushes his work throughout, gives rise to effects we look for rather from music than from verse. And there is, as in music, a sequence, seeming necessary and yet unforeseen, of feeling, acting often with magical strokes (*e.g.*, in *Love's Consolation*, "Ah, God! Thy lightnings should have wakened me three days before they did;" in *Mano*, "She would have answered underneath the boughs").

'He is faulty by a certain vagueness of form, some unpleasing rhymes, and most by an obscurity—partly of thought, partly of expression—suggesting a deeper meaning behind the text without leaving the reader any decisive clue to find it. This fault injures the general effect of *Mano*. He employs

177

sometimes the archaic style now common, but with such a mastery and dramatic point as justify a practice otherwise vicious.'

NOTE L, *page* 127. *The Academy*, 22 November 1884, a review of *Prometheus* in 1½ columns, by J. W. Mackail, praises not only its 'freshness, lucidity, delicacy', but also its 'sustained power, and a mastery of rhythm and language almost of the first rank'. It . . . 'comes nearer, perhaps, to the Greek spirit and tone than any English play that has been written since Milton'. The writer notes the influences of the choruses in *Samson Agonistes*.

APPENDIX

COMPARATIVE NUMBERING OF THE POEMS IN THE SECOND AND THIRD EDITIONS WHEN DIFFERENCES OCCUR.

Poem	Number in 2nd edition	Number in 3rd edition
For a Picture of St Dorothea	1	19
Heaven Haven	2	20
The Habit of Perfection	3	24
The Wreck of the Deutschland	4	28
The Silver Jubilee	6	30
God's Grandeur	7	31
The Starlight Night	8	32
Spring	9	33
The Lantern Out of Doors	10	34
The Sea and the Skylark	11	35
The Windhover	12	36
Pied Beauty	13	37
Hurrahing in Harvest	14	38
The Caged Skylark	15	39
In the Valley of the Elwy	16	40
The Loss of the Eurydice	17	41
The May Magnificat	18	42
Binsey Poplars	19	43
Duns Scotus's Oxford	20	44
Henry Purcell	21	45
Peace	22	46
The Bugler's First Communion	23	47
Morning Midday and Evening Sacrifice	24	48
Andromeda	25	49
The Candle Indoors	26	50
The Handsome Heart	27	51
At the Wedding March	28	52
Felix Randall	29	53
Brothers	30	54
Spring and Fall	31	55
Spelt from Sybil's Leaves	32	62
Inversnaid	33	56
'As kingfishers catch fire, dragonflies draw flame'	34	57

Appendix

INDEX

All musical matters, including the names of composers, are indexed under 'Music'.
All matters relating to the technicalities of poetry are indexed under 'Versification'.
The page-numbers in parentheses indicate indirect or associated allusions.

Index

Burton, Sir R., i. 321.
Butler, Alban, i. 40.
Byrne, Graham, i. 126.
Byron, i. 225, ii. 65, 98–9.

Caesar, ii. 137.
Caine, [Sir] T. Hall, i. 124; and R. B., i.
  129,134,215,272; and Rossetti,i. 162,
  169,172, ii. 7,105; Sonnet-anthology,
  i. 127–8, 132, 162, ii. 46–7, 49, 51; on
  'unity of action', ii. 110.
Campbell, T., i. 45, ii. 13, 14, 17, 23,
  99; G. M. H.'s setting of 'Battle of the
  Baltic', i. 201–2, 207, 219, 240, ii.
  170.
Campion, Edmund, i. 135, 147, 150, ii.
  76, 92, 94.
'Canonical beauty', ii. 83.
Carlisle, i. 140, 143, ii. 29, 52, 58–60,
  69, 91, 103–4, 153.
Carlyle, i. 27, ii. 17, 51–2, 59, 60, 75.
Caroline poets, i. 82, 101.
Cassidys, the, i. 268, ii. 150.
'Castalian', ii. 84 (cf. 'Parnassian').
Castle of Otranto, i. 228.
Catholic Church, Roman: Catholic
  commentators, i. 177; conversions to,
  i. 2–10, 14–17, 28, 40, 60, 88, 135–6,
  232; doctrines, i. 62, 77, 95, 149, 163,
  171, 186–8; expressions, i. 222;
  practices, i. 33, 62, 124, 133, 147–8,
  151, 194, 222; sympathies, i. 65, 90,
  136, 148, 177, 223; traditions, i. 53.
Catholic epistles, i. 195.
Catholicism, G. M. H.'s, i. 163, 170.
Catullus, i. 232.
Celtic languages, i. 165.
Century Magazine, The, i. 192.
Cervantes, ii. 140.
Challis, H. W., i. 2, 3, 19, 23.
Channing, W. E., ii. 18.
Chaucer, i. 107–8, 121, 320, ii. 66–7,
  78, 92, 156.
Chess, i. 187, ii. 79.
Chesterfield, i. 47, 86, 106.
Cholmeley School, Highgate, ii. 1.
Christ, i. 66, 73, 78, 175, 177, 188, 231,
  287, ii. 3, 5, 8, 9, 93, 137.
Christianity, i. 60–1, 186, 287–8, 298,
  302.
Chrysostom, St., i. 177.
Cicero, i. 247 n. 1, 267, 302.
Clare, —, S.J., ii. 62.
Clarke, W. A., i. 9.
Classical Review, i. 255, 266, 270, 277.
Clement of Rome, St., i. 195.
Clongowes, i. 191, 203, ii. 10 n.
Cobbett, W., ii. 96, 100, 103.

Coleridge, i. 250, ii. 177; on prosody, ii.
  18, 173; principles of criticism, ii.
  121; Christabel, ii. 18, 21, 173.
Coles, V. S. S., i. 1, 3, 11, 16, 29, 88,
  307.
Collins, J. C., i. 243 n. 1.
— W., 'Ode to Evening', i. 199, 202,
  211, 214.
Colonial Exhibition (1886), ii. 131.
Colours, ii. 38, 61.
Comfort, R., i. 205.
Commeline, A., i. 184.
Communism, i. 27, 29, (272–4).
Connemara, i. 193.
Constable, John, i. 154.
Contemporary Review, i. 171, ii. 110.
Cornhill Magazine, i. 42, ii. 10.
Corpus Christi, i. 147–9.
Cory, W. Johnson, i. 14, 29, 85, 98.
Cowper, W., ii. 63.
Crabbe, G., ii. 99.
Crawley, R., i. 132, 225–6.
Creighton, Mandell, ii. 137 n. 2.
Croke, Archbishop, i. (223), 252.
Croydon, i. 22, ii. 167.
Cuckoo's Song, i. 145–6.
'Cultshah', i. 130.
Curtis, R., S.J., i. 216 n. 2, 278, 319.

'Damfooling', i. (41), 129, 172, 174.
Dana, Two Years before the Mast, i. 279.
Daniel, Rev. C. H., i. 173, 176, 192, 275,
  302–3, ii. 107 n. 2, 120–1, 131, 138.
Dante, i. 225.
Dargle, the, i. 241.
Darlington, Rev. J., S.J., i. 216 n. 2.
Darwinism, i. 172, 281, 290.
Davis, a gardener, i. 145.
Demosthenes, i. 268.
De Quincey, i. 51.
De Vere, Aubrey, i. 280, ii. 112.
Devonshire, ii. 167.
Dialect, i. 87–8.
Dickens, David Copperfield, ii. 151; Edwin
  Drood (Mrs. Sapsea's Epitaph), i. 248;
  Old Curiosity Shop, i. 279; Our Mutual
  Friend, i. 174, ii. 153; pathos, ii. 73;
  Pecksniff, i. 199.
Didcot, i. 224.
Dillon, John, i. 252.
Disraeli, i. 304, ii. 71.
Dixon, R. W. I. Personally. His Angli-
  canism, ii. 31, 49, 51, 96; and T. Hall
  Caine, i. 127–8; a carriage accident,
  ii. 9, 12, 27; daughters, ii. 89, 91, 100;
  and fame (s.v. Fame); his first wife, ii.
  171; a gentleman, i. 139, 176; ill-
  health, ii. 16; and the Jesuits, ii. 176;

Index

Index

Index

Index

Index